Parties & Potluck Entertaining

Paré • Darcy

Library and Archives Canada Cataloguing in Publication

Paré, Jean, author
Parties and potluck entertaining / Jean Paré, James Darcy.

Includes index.
ISBN 978-1-988133-42-3 (softcover)

1. Entertaining. 2. Parties. 3. Cooking. 4. Cookbooks.
I. Darcy, James, author II. Title.

TX731.P736 2017 642'.4 C2017-903374-3

Cover photo: MarynaVoronova/Thinkstock

All inside photos are by Company's Coming Publishing except:
p. 4 (rez-art), p. 6 (Shaiith), p. 10 (martiapunts), p. 16 (OksanaKiian), p. 22 (katyenka), p. 30, Mizina, p. 34 (darrenplatts123), p. 38 (hatman12), p. 40 (Anna_Shepulova), p. 42 (rez-art), p. 46 (sea_and_trees), p. 58 (ginauf), p. 60 (SherSor), p. 66 (pramecomix), p. 80 (Delpixart), p. 84 (ALLEKO), p. 114 (jenifoto), p. 120 (nata_vkusidey), p. 124 (SherSor), p. 126 (AlexRaths), p. 128 (tataks), p. 136 (leaf), p. 152 (Paul_Brighton), p. 154 (ginauf), p. 156 (bart4u).

Distributed by
Canada Book Distributors - Booklogic
11414-119 Street
Edmonton. Alberta, Canada T5G 2X6
Tel: 1-800-661-9017

We acknowledge the financial support of the Government of Canada.
Nous reconnaissons l'appui financier du gouvernement du Canada.

PC: 38

Table of Contents

Practical Gourmet

Good company and great food are a powerful combination. When laughter and conversation mix with the heady fragrance and flavours of delicious fare, we are not just sharing a meal—we are nourishing our lives. Artfully prepared dishes awaken the senses and please the palate. And here's the secret: It can be so simple!

Practical Gourmet is delighted to collaborate with **Company's Coming** to introduce a new series designed to help home cooks create no-fuss, sumptuous food. It is possible to wow both the eye and the palate using readily available ingredients and minimal effort. Practical Gourmet offers recipes without the hassle of complicated methods, special equipment or obscure ingredients.

Titles in this series feature step-by-step instructions, full-page colour photos with every recipe, menu suggestions and sidebars on preparation tips and tricks.

Approachable recipes, fabulous results, wonderful get-togethers—it all starts with *Parties & Potluck Entertaining!*

The Jean Paré Story

Jean Paré (pronounced "jeen PAIR-ee") grew up understanding that the combination of family, friends and home cooking is the best recipe for a good life. When Jean left home, she took with her a love of cooking, many family recipes and an intriguing desire to read cookbooks as if they were novels!

When her four children had all reached school age, Jean volunteered to cater the 50th anniversary celebration of the Vermilion School of Agriculture, now Lakeland College, in Alberta, Canada. Working from her home, Jean prepared a dinner for more than 1,000 people and from there launched a flourishing catering operation that continued for more than 18 years.

As requests for her recipes increased, Jean was often asked, "Why don't you write a cookbook?" The release of *150 Delicious Squares* on April 14, 1981, marked the debut of what would soon turn into one of the world's most popular cookbook series.

"Never share a recipe you wouldn't use yourself."

Company's Coming cookbooks are distributed in Canada, the United States, Australia and other world markets. Bestsellers many times over in English, Company's Coming cookbooks have also been published in French and Spanish.

Familiar and trusted in home kitchens around the world, Jean's recipes are offered in a variety of formats by Practical Gourmet. Highly regarded as kitchen workbooks, the softcover Original Series, with its lay-flat plastic comb binding, is still a favourite among home cooks.

Jean Paré's approach to cooking has always called for quick and easy recipes using everyday ingredients. That view served her well, and the tradition continues in the Practical Gourmet series.

Jean's Golden Rule of Cooking is: Never share a recipe you wouldn't use yourself. It's an approach that has worked—millions of times over!

Introduction

Parties don't have to be formal affairs. Anytime you have a get-together with friends or family and food, it's a party. No matter what the occasion, whenever hungry people gather, potluck is a fun, easy way to entertain a few or feed a crowd. Everyone makes a little; everyone enjoys a lot; and no one spends all day in the kitchen.

Whether you're the host of the event or an invited guest, *Parties and Potluck Entertaining* puts everything you need at your fingertips. From appetizers to desserts, we offer delicious recipes for the many occasions during the year when people come together to celebrate. These pages are also filled with helpful preparation and entertaining tips, and we've included Potluck Suggestions to indicate just how far a dish will stretch.

Tips for the Potluck Host

Potluck can be an intriguing combination of food and luck, where guests share whatever they happen to bring. Going that route and just leaving it to chance can be fun, as long as you are aware that you run the risk of dining on nothing but a variety of salads or desserts. If you want to ensure your guests will be getting a more rounded nosh-up, assign each guest a type of dish to bring (appetizer, side, dessert, etc.), or send out a sign-up sheet so people can see what other guests are bringing and choose for themselves what they would like to contribute.

If any of your guests have dietary restrictions, let the other guests know so they can make an informed choice when deciding what dish they would like to bring.

Provide pens or markers and blank labels or sticky notes so people can label their food as they put it on the table. You could even encourage them to write a little description of the dish, so people know what to expect.

Remember to keep hot foods hot, and cold foods cold. The last thing you want to do is give your guests food poisoning, so make sure you keep food at the proper temperature to prevent the growth of food-borne bacteria (at least 165°F [73°C] for hot foods and below 40°F [4°C] for cold foods). As your guests arrive, put the hot foods into a warm oven, if possible, and the cold foods into the fridge until you are ready to serve them.

If you are hosting a potluck outside of your home, check out the on-site amenities before the day of the potluck. Is there a fridge, or will you have to rely on coolers? Will you have access to stoves or microwaves? Are there bathrooms, and are they well stocked, or should you bring the necessities with you?

Tips for the Potluck Guest

If you are invited to a potluck, there are a few things you should keep in mind when deciding what dish to bring.

Potluck foods should not be fussy. There should be little or no last minute preparation. The kitchen will be busy enough, so don't add to the chaos by bringing a dish that needs a lot of finishing on site. If items need to be garnished, sliced or cut, make those final preparations at home.

Potluck dishes should, however, be relatively hearty. The food will likely be sitting out for a while, so choose a dish that will hold up well on the table.

Arrive with your food at the proper temperature. Don't bring your dish expecting that you will be able to use the host's oven or microwave.

If you are unsure of how much food to bring, consider how many guests will be attending. For large potlucks, there will be many dishes to choose from, so you can expect people to take just a small sampling of each. For smaller potlucks, there will be fewer dishes to choose from, so people will take a bigger portion of each.

Remember to bring serving utensils appropriate for your dish, label your utensils, serving dishes or appliances with your name. If you are bringing your food in a slow cooker, don't forget an extension cord.

The many dishes in this book are ideal for occasions throughout the year. We know you will find a dish that will become a favourite for many the potlucks (or nosh-ups) you attend, whether you are the host or a guest.

Brunch Dish

Loaded with bacon, green pepper and two kinds of cheese, this casserole is the perfect pick-me-up brunch dish after a night of New Year's indulgence.

Bacon slices, diced	**6**	**6**
Chopped green pepper	**1/4 cup**	**60 mL**
Chopped onion	**1/4 cup**	**60 mL**
Frozen hash brown potatoes, thawed	**2 cups**	**500 mL**
Large eggs	**4**	**4**
Water	**1/4 cup**	**60 mL**
Salt	**1/2 tsp.**	**2 mL**
Pepper	**1/8 tsp.**	**0.5 mL**
Grated medium Cheddar cheese	**1/2 cup**	**125 mL**
Grated part-skim mozzarella cheese	**1/2 cup**	**125 mL**
Chopped fresh parsley, for garnish		

Combine first 3 ingredients in large non-stick frying pan on medium. Cook for 5 to 10 minutes, stirring often, until bacon is crisp. Remove with slotted spoon to paper towel to drain. Drain all but 1 tbsp. (15 mL) drippings from pan.

Press hash browns evenly in same frying pan. Cook, uncovered, for about 10 minutes on medium-low, stirring occasionally, until crisp.

Beat next 4 ingredients in small bowl. Add bacon mixture. Stir. Pour over hash browns.

Sprinkle with half of Cheddar and mozzarella. Cook for about 5 minutes, stirring occasionally, until almost set. Turn oven to broil with rack in middle. Remove casserole from pan and place in 8 x 8 inch (20 x 20 cm) baking dish. Sprinkle with remaining cheese and broil for 5 minutes. Garnish with parsley. Serves 6.

Scottish Meat Pie

Haggis is the dish traditionally served on Robbie Burns Day, but it might not be to everyone's liking, so if you want to play it safe, offer your guests this meat pie instead. Scottish meat pies were originally made with mutton, but we like the flavour combination of pork and beef or lamb. The whisky cream sauce is optional but gives the pie a real Scottish flair.

Butter	2/3 cup	150 mL
Hot water	1 cup	250 mL
All-purpose flour	4 1/2 cups	1.1 L
Baking powder	1 tbsp.	15 mL
Salt	2 tsp.	10 mL
Butter	1 1/3 cups	325 mL
Large egg	1	1
Lemon juice	1 tbsp.	15 mL
Butter	2 tbsp.	30 mL
Medium yellow onions, diced	4	4
Ground pork	1 lb.	500 g
Ground beef or lamb	1 lb.	500 g
Large baking potatoes, grated	2	2
Minced garlic	1 tbsp.	15 mL
Red wine	1 1/2 cups	375 mL
Chopped fresh rosemary	2 tbsp.	30 mL
Balsamic vinegar	1/4 cup	60 mL
Ground allspice	1 tsp.	5 mL
Ground cinnamon	1 tsp.	5 mL
Large egg, fork beaten	1	1

Combine first amount of butter and hot water in a bowl, stirring until butter has melted. Set aside to cool.

Combine next 3 ingredients in a food processor. Add second amount of butter and pulse until mixture resembles coarse meal.

Whisk first egg and lemon juice into butter and water mixture and pour into processor, pulsing until just coming together. Form into 2 discs, one slightly larger than other. Wrap and chill for at least 2 hours.

Heat remaining butter in a large pot. Add onion and cook until browned. Add both meats and brown, stirring to break up clumps.

Add next 7 ingredients and simmer, uncovered, for 20 minutes or until starting to thicken. Remove from heat and set aside to cool.

Roll out larger disk and line a 9 inch (23 cm) springform pan. Brush pastry with egg wash and pour in cooled filling. Cover with top crust. Slash top to allow steam to escape, brush with egg wash and bake in 375°F (190°C) oven until golden brown, 30 to 40 minutes. Makes 8 servings.

Potluck suggestion: Can serve up to 12.

To make a whisky cream sauce, heat 2 cups (500 ml) whipping cream in a pan over medium heat. Add 2 tsp. (10 mL) whisky and 2 tsp. (10 mL) wholegrain mustard and stir to combine. Bring mixture to a simmer and cook for 1 to 2 minutes. Remove from heat and stir in 1 tbsp. (15 mL) chopped chives and 2 tsp. (10 mL) lemon juice. Season with salt and pepper, to taste.

Scallops Arrabiata

Add a little spice to your night with this classy dish. Perfect for a dinner party for two.

Bacon slices, chopped	**4**	**4**
Large sea scallops	**1 lb.**	**454 g**
Can of diced tomatoes (with juice) (14 oz., 398 mL)	**1**	**1**
White wine vinegar	**1 tbsp.**	**15 mL**
Garlic clove, minced (or 1/4 tsp., 1 mL, powder)	**1**	**1**
Dried crushed chilies	**1/2 tsp.**	**2 mL**
Granulated sugar	**1/4 tsp.**	**1 mL**
Salt	**1/8 tsp.**	**0.5 mL**
Pepper	**1/8 tsp.**	**0.5 mL**
Finely shredded basil	**1 tbsp.**	**15 mL**

Cook bacon in a large frying pan on medium until crisp. Transfer with a slotted spoon to a plate lined with paper towel to drain. Drain and discard all but 2 tsp. (10 mL) drippings.

Add scallops to same frying pan. Cook for about 1 minute per side until browned. Remove to a large plate.

Add next 7 ingredients to same frying pan. Cook for 5 minutes, stirring occasionally. Add scallops and bacon. Heat, stirring, for about 2 minutes until scallops are opaque.

Sprinkle with basil. Makes 2 servings.

If you would like to add the romance of a candle-lit dinner to your evening but don't really want candles on your table, try replacing your ordinary light bulbs with coloured ones. Choose a soft, romantic colour to set the perfect mood.

Mocha Layer Cake

Set the mood for the evening with this sumptuous, sensual chocolate masterpiece. Rich without being heavy, it is everything you'd want in a Valentine's Day dessert.

All-purpose flour	**1 3/4 cups**	**425 mL**
Granulated sugar	**1 cup**	**250 mL**
Baking soda	**1 tsp.**	**5 mL**
Salt	**1/2 tsp.**	**2 mL**
Hot strong prepared coffee	**1 cup**	**250 mL**
Cocoa, sifted if lumpy	**1/2 cup**	**125 mL**
1% buttermilk	**1/2 cup**	**125 mL**
Egg whites (about 2 large)	**1/4 cup**	**60 mL**
Vanilla extract	**1 tsp.**	**5 mL**
Cold strong prepared coffee	**1 cup**	**250 mL**
Box of instant fat-free chocolate pudding powder (4-serving size)	**1**	**1**
Frozen 95% fat-free whipped topping, thawed	**3 cups**	**750 mL**

Line bottom of two 8 inch (20 cm) round pans with parchment paper circles. Spray sides with cooking spray. Set aside. Combine first 4 ingredients in a large bowl.

Whisk first amount of coffee and cocoa in a small bowl until cocoa is dissolved.

Combine next 3 ingredients in a medium bowl. Stir in coffee mixture. Add to flour mixture. Stir until just combined. Spread evenly in prepared pans. Bake in 350°F (175°C) oven for about 20 minutes until wooden pick inserted in centre of cake comes out clean. Let stand in pans for 10 minutes before inverting onto wire racks to cool completely. Cut each cake in half horizontally to make 4 layers.

For the frosting, beat second amount of coffee and pudding powder in a medium bowl for 2 minutes. Add 1 cup (250 mL) whipped topping. Stir until combined. Fold in remaining whipped topping. Chill for 30 minutes. Place 1 cake layer on a serving plate. Spread with about 1/2 cup (125 mL) frosting. Repeat with second and third cake layers, spreading about 1/2 cup (125 mL) frosting between each layer. Cover with remaining cake layer. Spread remaining frosting over top and sides of cake. Chill for at least 1 hour. Cuts into 8 wedges.

Potluck suggestion: Can cut into up to 12 wedges.

Banana Maple Pecan Pancakes

Mardi Gras *translates as Fat Tuesday in English, and yet to the English the day is known as Shrove Tuesday or Pancake Tuesday. It is the last day before Ash Wednesday and the 40 days of abstinence of Lent. Lent meant doing without, so Mardi Gras became a time to indulge in the rich foods such as butter, sugar, milk and eggs that had to be used up before the Lenten penance. Today people add a range of berries, fruit, chocolate and maple syrup to their pancake feast.*

Ingredient	Imperial	Metric
All-purpose flour	**2 cups**	**500 mL**
Chopped pecans, toasted (see sidebar, page 70)	**1/2 cup**	**125 mL**
Baking powder		
Ground cinnamon	**1/4 tsp.**	**1 mL**
Salt	**1/4 tsp.**	**1 mL**
Diced overripe banana	**1 1/2 cups**	**375 mL**
Milk	**1 3/4 cups**	**425 mL**
Maple syrup	**1/4 cup**	**60 mL**
Cooking oil	**2 tbsp.**	**30 mL**

Combine first 5 ingredients in a large bowl. Make a well in centre.

Mash half of banana in a medium bowl. Add remaining 3 ingredients and mix until smooth. Stir in remaining banana. Add to well. Stir just until combined. Batter will be lumpy. Preheat electric griddle to medium-high. Spray griddle with cooking spray. Pour batter onto griddle, using 1/4 cup (60 mL) for each pancake. Cook for about 3 minutes until bubbles form on top and edges appear dry. Flip pancake and cook for about 2 minutes until bottom is golden. Transfer to a plate. Cover to keep warm. Repeat with remaining batter, spraying griddle with more cooking spray if necessary to prevent sticking. Makes about 15 pancakes.

The Pancake Tuesday Race, which dates back to 1445, is held in many communities throughout the United Kingdom, particularly in England and several of its colonies. During the event, participants wear aprons and hats or scarves as they race down the main street carrying a frying pan and spatula to flip their pancake.

Irish Lentil Stew with Hearty Irish Soda Bread

A warm, rustic stew that is the perfect dish for a St. Patrick's Day potluck. Pair it with this golden loaf full of sweet raisins for an authentic Irish meal.

Cooking oil	2 tsp.	10 mL
Boneless lamb shoulder, trimmed of fat and cut into 1 inch (2.5 cm) pieces	1 1/2 lbs.	680 g
Garlic powder	1/2 tsp.	2 mL
Pepper	1/4 tsp.	1 mL
Chopped onion	2 cups	500 mL
Guinness Draught	1 cup	250 mL
Low-sodium prepared chicken broth	3 cups	750 mL
Red baby potatoes, larger ones cut in half	1 1/2 lbs.	680 g
Baby carrots	2 cups	500 mL
Chopped celery	1 1/2 cups	375 mL
Dried green lentils	1 cup	250 mL
Dried thyme	1/2 tsp.	2 mL
Bay leaf	1	1
Chopped fresh parsley	2 tbsp.	30 mL
All-purpose flour	1 1/2 cups	375 mL
Whole wheat flour	1 1/2 cups	375 mL
Dark raisins	1/2 cup	125 mL
Wheat germ, toasted	1/4 cup	60 mL
Brown sugar, packed	2 tbsp.	30 mL
Baking soda	1 1/2 tsp.	7 mL
Caraway seed	1 tsp.	5 mL
Salt	3/4 tsp.	4 mL
1% buttermilk	1 1/2 cups	375 mL
Low-fat plain yogurt	1/2 cup	125 mL
Canola oil	1/4 cup	60 mL

Heat oil in a Dutch oven on medium-high. Add lamb and sprinkle with garlic powder and pepper. Cook for about 10 minutes, stirring occasionally, until browned.

Add onion and Guinness. Heat, stirring, for 1 minute, scraping any brown bits from bottom of pot.

Stir in next 7 ingredients and bring to a boil. Reduce heat to medium-low and simmer, covered, for about 2 hours, stirring occasionally, until lamb is tender. Remove and discard bay leaf. Sprinkle with parsley. Makes about 9 cups (2.25 L).

For the bread, combine next 8 ingredients in a large bowl and make a well in centre.

Combine next 3 ingredients in a small bowl. Add to well and stir until just moistened. Spread evenly in a greased 9 x 5 x 3 inch (23 x 12.5 x 7.5 cm) loaf pan. Bake in 350°F (175°C) oven for about 50 minutes until wooden pick inserted in centre comes out clean. Let stand in pan for 10 minutes before removing to a wire rack to cool. Cuts into 16 slices.

To toast wheat germ, spread it evenly in an ungreased shallow frying pan and heat, stirring, on medium until golden. Or it spread evenly in an ungreased shallow pan and bake in a 350°F (175°C) oven for 3 minutes, stirring or shaking often, until golden. Cool before adding to the recipe.

Parkerhouse Pockets

A St. Patrick's Day spread is not complete without some sort of potato on offer, and these soft potato rolls fit the bill. Filled with a creamy mixture of cheese and green onion, these rolls make a great snack all on their own or pair wonderfully with a bowl of piping hot soup or a fresh green salad.

Light ricotta cheese	**1 cup**	**250 mL**
Green onions, finely sliced	**4**	**4**
Skim milk	**1 1/4 cups**	**300 mL**
Small peeled potato, cooked and mashed	**1**	**1**
Granulated sugar	**1/3 cup**	**75 mL**
Canola oil	**1/4 cup**	**60 mL**
Salt	**3/4 tsp.**	**4 mL**
Whole wheat flour	**2 cups**	**500 mL**
Envelope of instant yeast (1/4 oz., 8 g) (or 2 1/4 tsp., 11 mL)	**1**	**1**
Egg white (large)	**1**	**1**
All-purpose flour	**2 cups**	**500 mL**
All-purpose flour, approximately	**1/2 cup**	**125 mL**

Combine cheese and green onion in a small bowl. Set aside.

Combine next 5 ingredients in a small saucepan. Heat, stirring, on medium until sugar is dissolved. Cool until warm.

Combine whole wheat flour and yeast in an extra-large bowl. Stir in potato mixture until you have a thick batter consistency. Add egg white. Mix well.

Add first amount of all-purpose flour, 1/2 cup (125 mL) at a time, until a soft dough forms. Turn out onto a lightly floured surface and knead for 5 to 10 minutes, adding second amount of all-purpose flour 1 tbsp. (15 mL) at a time, if necessary, to prevent sticking, until smooth and elastic (you might not need the entire 1/2 cup, 125 mL). Place in a greased extra-large bowl, turning once to grease top. Cover with greased wax paper and a tea towel. Let stand in oven with light on and door closed for about 15 minutes until doubled in bulk. Punch dough down. Cut dough in half. Roll one portion out on a lightly floured surface to 1/2 inch (12 mm) thickness. Cut with a 3 inch (7 cm) round cutter. Place 1 tsp. (5 mL) cheese mixture in middle of round. Fold dough over filling. Pinch edges firmly together to seal. Repeat with remaining dough and filling. Arrange on 2 large greased baking sheets. Cover with greased wax paper and a tea towel. Let stand in oven with light on and door closed for about 40 minutes until doubled in size. Bake, uncovered, on separate racks, in 350°F (175°C) oven for 20 to 25 minutes, switching position of baking sheets at halftime, until golden brown. Makes 24 pockets.

Curried Devilled Eggs

At your next Easter get-together, leave the coloured eggs for the children and treat your palate to these eggs instead. Chutney and curry give these devilled eggs a sweet and spicy flair that's a nice change from the usual version. If you like, add a sprinkle of paprika and a snippet of chive tips to each egg half just before serving.

Hard-boiled eggs, peeled	**6**	**6**
Mayonnaise	**1/4 cup**	**60 mL**
Mango chutney, any large pieces finely chopped	**1 tbsp.**	**15 mL**
Chopped fresh chives	**2 tsp.**	**10 mL**
Curry powder	**1/4 tsp.**	**1 mL**
Salt, to taste		
Pepper, to taste		

Cut eggs in half lengthwise. Remove egg yolks to a small bowl. Set egg white halves aside. Mash egg yolks until no lumps remain.

Add remaining 6 ingredients to egg yolk and mix until well combined. Spoon 1 tbsp. (15 mL) into each egg white half. Place in an airtight container lined with paper towel.

Chill for 2 hours or overnight. Makes 12 devilled eggs.

To make your devilled eggs even more attractive, scoop the egg yolk mixture into a pastry bag or resealable freezer bag with the corner snipped off and pipe it into the egg white halves instead of using a spoon.

White Bean and Basil Cones

These rich, savoury cones will elevate your Easter spread with their wonderful combination of Parmesan, basil and lemon. The optional smoked salmon and chives add a little splash of colour and depth of flavour, but the cones are equally delicious without them. If you don't have time to make your own Parmesan cones, you could substitute waffle cones for a slightly different, sweeter taste sensation. This dish doesn't travel well so it best reserved for a potluck where you are the host, not a guest.

Grated fresh Parmesan cheese	**3/4 cup**	**175 mL**
Pepper	**1/4 tsp.**	**1 mL**
Canned white kidney beans, rinsed and drained	**1 cup**	**250 mL**
Basil pesto	**1 tbsp.**	**15 mL**
Lemon juice	**2 tsp.**	**10 mL**
Olive oil	**2 tsp.**	**10 mL**
Smoked salmon slices, thinly sliced (optional)	**5**	**5**
Finely chopped chives (optional)	**2 tbsp**	**30 mL**

Cut two 3 1/2 inch (9 cm) diameter circles from heavy paper. Shape into cones and tape or staple securely. Place a sheet of parchment paper on a baking sheet and trace two 3 1/2 inch (9 cm) diameter circles, about 3 inches (7.5 cm) apart. Turn paper over. Combine cheese and pepper and spread about 1 tbsp. (15 mL) cheese mixture over each circle. Bake in 350°F (175°C) oven for about 5 minutes until melted and golden. Let stand for 1 minute and then transfer to a plate. Immediately place 1 paper cone on cheese and roll around cone. Repeat with second cheese round and cone. Let stand until cool. Wipe parchment paper to remove any crumbs and repeat with remaining cheese mixture.

In a blender or food processor, process next 4 ingredients until smooth. Stir in remaining 2 ingredients. Spoon into a piping bag or small freezer bag with 1 corner snipped off and pipe into cones. Serve immediately. Makes about 10 cones.

Don't cheat yourself by using powdered Parmesan. Grate the fresh stuff for a truly magnificent flavour and perfect results.

Fruity Lamb Tagine

Lamb is one of the meats traditionally eaten at Easter, but some people may find the thought of preparing lamb a bit intimidating. It need not be. This sweet lamb stew is easy to prepare and wonderfully satisfying. It will get rave reviews from your guests. This tagine is saucy enough to serve over couscous or brown basmati rice.

Ingredient	Imperial	Metric
All-purpose flour	**2 tbsp.**	**30 mL**
Salt	**1/4 tsp.**	**1 mL**
Pepper	**1/4 tsp.**	**1 mL**
Boneless lamb shoulder, trimmed of fat and cut into 1 inch (2.5 cm) pieces	**1 1/2 lbs.**	**680 g**
Cooking oil	**2 tsp.**	**10 mL**
Coarsely chopped onion	**1 1/2 cups**	**375 mL**
Ground coriander	**1 tsp.**	**5 mL**
Ground cumin	**1 tsp.**	**5 mL**
Garlic cloves, minced	**2**	**2**
Ground cinnamon	**1/2 tsp.**	**2 mL**
Cayenne pepper	**1/8 tsp.**	**0.5 mL**
Can of diced tomatoes (with juice) (14 oz., 398 mL)	**1**	**1**
Prepared chicken broth	**1 1/4 cups**	**300 mL**
Coarsely chopped dried apricot	**1/2 cup**	**125 mL**
Coarsely chopped pitted dates	**1/2 cup**	**125 mL**
Sliced natural almonds, toasted (see sidebar, page 70)	**1/4 cup**	**60 mL**

Combine first 3 ingredients in a large resealable freezer bag. Add lamb and toss until coated. Transfer lamb to a greased 2 quart (2 L) casserole.

Heat cooking oil in a large frying pan on medium. Add next 6 ingredients and cook for about 5 minutes, stirring often, until onion starts to soften.

Add tomatoes and broth. Heat, scraping any brown bits from bottom of pan, until boiling. Add to lamb.

Stir in apricot and dates. Cook, covered, in 325°F (160°C) oven for about 90 minutes until lamb is tender.

Scatter almonds over top. Makes about 8 cups (2 L).

Potluck suggestion: can serve up to 16.

Ham and Pasta Bake

This is a great option for an Easter potluck; you get a little taste of the traditional Easter ham plus a healthy dose of vegetables in one convenient, portable dish! After Easter, it is also a great way to use up some of the leftover ham from your Easter dinner.

Elbow macaroni	**2 cups**	**500 mL**
All-purpose flour	**1/4 cup**	**60 mL**
Onion flakes	**1 tbsp.**	**15 mL**
Dry mustard	**1/2 tsp.**	**2 mL**
Salt	**1 tsp.**	**5 mL**
Pepper	**1/8 tsp.**	**0.5 mL**
Milk	**2 1/2 cups**	**625 mL**
Chopped cooked broccoli	**3 cups**	**750 mL**
Diced cooked ham	**2 cups**	**500 mL**
Grated medium (or sharp) Cheddar cheese	**3/4 cup**	**175 mL**
Butter (or hard margarine)	**2 tbsp.**	**30 mL**
Fine dry bread crumbs	**1/2 cup**	**125 mL**

Cook macaroni in boiling salted water in a large uncovered saucepan or Dutch oven for 8 to 10 minutes, stirring occasionally, until tender but firm. Drain. Transfer to a greased 3 quart (3 L) casserole and set aside.

Combine next 5 ingredients in same saucepan.

Slowly add milk, stirring constantly until smooth. Heat, stirring, on medium for 10 to 15 minutes until boiling and thickened. Pour over macaroni.

Stir in next 3 ingredients.

Melt butter in a small saucepan. Remove from heat and stir in bread crumbs. Sprinkle over macaroni mixture. Bake, uncovered, in 350°F (175°C) oven for about 40 minutes until golden and bubbling at edges. Makes 6 servings.

Potluck suggestion: Can serve up to 12.

Roasted Vegetables with Aioli

Roasted veggies pair well with any meat dish and will be a welcome side at an Easter dinner or potluck. The aioli, a rich garlic mayonnaise, elevates these veggies from delicious to phenomenal. You can make the aioli a day or several hours ahead of serving time. Keep it refrigerated in a sealable container, and remove it from the fridge 30 minutes before serving.

Cauiflower florets	**2 cups**	**500mL**
Baby potatoes, halved	**10**	**10**
Medium carrots, peeled, halved lengthwise and chopped into 2 inch (5 cm) lengths	**6**	**6**
Medium red onions, quartered	**3**	**3**
Medium red peppers, quartered	**3**	**3**
Olive (or cooking) oil	**2 tbsp.**	**30 mL**
Salt	**1/2 tsp.**	**2 mL**
Pepper	**1/2 tsp.**	**2 mL**
Medium zucchini, halved lengthwise and chopped into 2 inch (5 cm) lengths	**6**	**6**
Garlic cloves	**7**	**7**
Egg yolks (large)	**2**	**2**
Lemon juice	**3 tbsp.**	**45 mL**
Salt	**1/4 tsp.**	**1 mL**
Light olive oil	**2 cups**	**500 mL**

Toss first 6 ingredients on an 11 x 17 inch (28 x 43 cm) baking sheet with sides. Bake in 350°F (175°C) oven for 30 minutes.

Stir in zucchini. Bake for about 25 minutes until vegetables are tender.

For the aioli, process next 4 ingredients in a food processor until well combined. With motor running, slowly pour olive oil through feed chute. Process until mixture is thick and pale. Serve over roasted vegetables. Makes 12 servings.

Lazy Daisy Cake

This old-fashioned favourite is perfect for a potluck because the golden coconut topping makes the cake much easier to transport than a cake topped with icing.

Large eggs	**2**	**2**
Granulated sugar	**1 cup**	**250 mL**
Vanilla	**1 tsp.**	**5 mL**
All-purpose flour	**1 cup**	**250 mL**
Baking powder	**1 tsp.**	**5 mL**
Salt	**1/2 tsp.**	**2 mL**
Milk	**1/2 cup**	**125 mL**
Butter (or hard margarine)	**1 tbsp.**	**15 mL**
Butter (or hard margarine)	**3 tbsp.**	**45 mL**
Brown sugar, packed	**1/2 cup**	**125 mL**
Half-and-half cream (or milk)	**2 tbsp.**	**30 mL**
Flake coconut	**1/2 cup**	**125 mL**

Beat eggs in a medium bowl until frothy. Add sugar, 2 tbsp. (30 mL) at a time while beating, until thickened. Add vanilla. Beat well.

Combine flour, baking powder and salt in a small bowl. Stir into egg mixture.

Heat milk and first amount of butter in a small heavy saucepan on medium, stirring, until butter is melted. Add to flour mixture. Stir well. Spread batter evenly in a greased 9 x 9 inch (23 x 23 cm) pan. Bake in 350°F (175°C) oven for 25 to 30 minutes until wooden pick inserted in centre comes out clean.

For the topping combine remaining butter, brown sugar and cream in a medium saucepan. Bring to a rolling boil on medium-high, stirring occasionally. Remove from heat.

Stir in coconut. Spread evenly over warm cake. Return to oven for about 3 minutes until top is bubbling. Let stand in pan on a wire rack until cool. Cuts into 12 pieces.

Potluck suggestion: Can cut into up to 16 pieces.

Hot Cross Buns

Easter wouldn't be Easter without hot cross buns. True, you can find commercial varieties on some supermarket shelves as early as January, but they cannot compare in taste or texture to homemade. Lightly spiced and filled with fruit, these rolls are the real deal. They will be the hit of the potluck.

Milk, scalded and cooled to lukewarm	**2 cups**	**500 mL**
Granulated sugar	**2 tsp.**	**10 mL**
Warm water	**1/2 cup**	**125 mL**
Packages active dry yeast (1/4 oz., 7 g, each)	**2**	**2**
All-purpose flour	**3 cups**	**750 mL**
Butter (or hard margarine), softened	**1/2 cup**	**125 mL**
Granulated sugar	**3/4 cup**	**175 mL**
Large eggs	**2**	**2**
Salt	**1 tsp.**	**5 mL**
Ground cinnamon	**1 tsp.**	**5 mL**
Ground nutmeg	**1/8 tsp.**	**0.5 mL**
Ground cloves	**1/8 tsp.**	**0.5 mL**
Currants or raisins	**1 cup**	**250 mL**
All-purpose flour	**3 1/2 cups**	**875 mL**
Butter (or hard margarine), softened	**2 tsp.**	**10 mL**
Icing (confectioner's) sugar	**1 cup**	**250 mL**
Milk	**1 tbsp.**	**15 mL**
Vanilla extract	**1/4 tsp.**	**1 mL**

Pour first amount of milk into a large bowl. Set aside.

Stir first amount of sugar into warm water in a small bowl. Sprinkle yeast over top. Let stand 10 minutes. Stir to dissolve yeast. Stir into milk.

Beat in first amount of flour until very smooth. Cover with greased waxed paper and a tea towel. Let stand in oven with light on and door closed for about 50 minutes until bubbly and light.

Cream first amount of butter and remaining sugar in another bowl. Beat in eggs 1 at a time. Stir in next 5 ingredients. Add to flour mixture. Work in enough remaining flour so that dough pulls away from sides of bowl. Turn out onto a floured surface. Knead about 5 minutes until smooth and elastic. Place dough in a greased bowl, turning once to grease top. Cover with a tea towel. Let stand in oven with light on and door closed for about 1 hour until doubled in size. Punch dough down. Divide into 3 equal portions. Divide each portion into 12 pieces. Shape into buns. Arrange in 3 greased

8 x 8 inch (20 x 20 cm) pans. Cover with a tea towel. Let stand in oven with light on and door closed for about 1 hour until doubled in size. Cut with scissors or slash with knife or razor blade to make a cross on top 1/8 inch (3 mm) deep. Bake in 375°F (190°C) oven for 12 to 15 minutes. Turn out onto racks. Brush warm tops with remaining butter. Set aside to cool.

For the glaze, mix icing sugar, milk and vanilla together to make a barely pourable glaze. Drizzle or pipe over slashes in cooled buns. Makes 36 buns.

Gingered Kale and Apple Salad

Show our planet a little love by throwing a "green" Earth Day potluck and celebrating Earth's natural resources and your commitment to protecting them. An ideal Earth Day dish should be simple to prepare and have a modest ecological footprint, and this salad fits the bill. Substitute the honey with your favourite vegan sweetener to make this dish vegan.

Decorative curly kale, trimmed of tough ribs	**2 lbs.**	**900 g**
Coarse sea salt	**1/4 cup**	**60 mL**
Rice vinegar	**1/4 cup**	**60 mL**
Small shallot, minced	**2**	**2**
Minced ginger root	**2 tbsp.**	**30 mL**
Raw honey	**4 tsp.**	**20 mL**
Finely grated lemon zest	**2 tsp.**	**10 mL**
Canola oil	**2 tbsp.**	**30 mL**
Sesame oil	**1 tbsp.**	**15 mL**
Salt, to taste		
Pepper, to taste		
Julienned apple (skin on)	**2 cups**	**500 mL**

Working in batches, stack kale leaves and cut diagonally into 1/4 inch (6 mm) wide strips. Transfer to a large bowl. Sprinkle with salt and toss to coat. Place a plate on top and add a weight on top of plate (such as a saucepan of water). Let stand for 15 minutes. Toss and replace plate and weight, and let stand for another 15 minutes. Drain and rinse several times. Transfer to a salad spinner and dry as much as possible.

Combine rice vinegar and shallot and let stand 15 minutes. Add ginger, honey and lemon zest and stir to combine. Drizzle in both oils, whisking constantly until well combined. Season with salt and pepper.

Combine kale and apple in a large bowl. Drizzle with dressing and toss to coat. Serve immediately or cover and refrigerate for up to 2 hours before serving. Makes 8 servings.

Potluck suggestion: Can serve up to 12.

Because different people have different food likes, dislikes and tolerances, it can be helpful to write the ingredients of the dish you are providing on an index card that can be displayed alongside your dish. Then other diners will know if they can add your offering to their plate or if they are best to avoid it.

Salsa Corn Tarts

Looking for the perfect appetizer to serve at your next Cinco de Mayo party? Try these crisp tortilla cups filled with cheese and corn custard, and topped with sour cream and avocado. Delicious!

Whole wheat flour tortillas (10 inch, 25 cm, diameter)	**3**	**3**
Grated Mexican cheese blend	**2/3 cup**	**150 mL**
Large eggs	**2**	**2**
Salsa	**1/2 cup**	**125 mL**
Chopped frozen kernel corn, thawed	**1/4 cup**	**60 mL**
Pepper	**1/4 tsp.**	**1 mL**
Sour cream	**1/4 cup**	**60 mL**
Finely diced avocado	**1/4 cup**	**60 mL**
Lime juice	**2 tsp.**	**10 mL**
Finely chopped cilantro (or fresh parsley)	**1 tbsp.**	**15 mL**

Cut twelve 4 inch (10 cm) rounds from tortillas. Press rounds into greased muffin cups. Bake in 400°F (200°C) oven for about 8 minutes until golden and crisp. Let stand for 15 minutes. Reduce heat to 350°F (175°C).

Sprinkle cheese into tortillas.

Whisk next 4 ingredients in small bowl and spoon over cheese. Bake for about 22 minutes until set.

Dollop sour cream over tarts. Toss avocado with lime juice in a small bowl and arrange over sour cream. Sprinkle with cilantro. Makes 12 tarts.

To spice up your potluck, choose a theme and ask everyone to bring along a dish and accompaniments that fit the mood. And have a little fun with it; get creative! For a Cinco de Mayo potluck, for example, go beyond the traditional tacos and guacamole; why not celebrate Mexican culture with an "authentic Mexican dish" potluck, or an "obscure Mexican ingredient" challenge, and ask people to bring along traditional Mexican music and wear the colours of the national flag.

Grilled Smoky Beef Empanadas

Celebrate Mexican culture with a staple of Mexican cuisine! Originally brought to Mexico by early Spanish explorers and settlers, the empanada has become a common and popular food throughout Mexico. It can be served for breakfast, as a snack, as a dessert or as a party food, depending on the filling. These empanadas are stuffed with ground beef, olives and raisins, a flavour combination reminiscent of the classic picadillo of Spain. Add a sprinkle of dried crushed chilies or cayenne pepper if you like a little more heat.

Ingredient	Imperial	Metric
Cooking oil	**1 tsp.**	**5 mL**
Extra-lean ground beef	**1 lb.**	**454 g**
Chopped onion	**1 1/2 cups**	**375 mL**
Ground cumin	**1 tsp.**	**5 mL**
Dried oregano	**1/2 tsp.**	**2 mL**
Salt	**1/4 tsp.**	**1 mL**
Pepper	**1/4 tsp.**	**1 mL**
Chopped raisins	**1/3 cup**	**75 mL**
Chopped green olives	**1/2 cup**	**125 mL**
Hickory barbecue sauce	**3 tbsp.**	**45 mL**
Red wine vinegar	**1 tbsp.**	**15 mL**
Garlic cloves, minced	**2**	**2**
Grated Mexican cheese blend	**1 1/2 cups**	**375 mL**
Frozen whole wheat dinner roll dough portions, covered, thawed in refrigerator overnight	**12**	**12**

Heat cooking oil in a large frying pan on medium. Add next 6 ingredients. Scramble-fry for about 8 minutes until beef is browned.

Add next 5 ingredients. Cook, stirring, for about 5 minutes until heated through. Remove from heat. Stir in cheese.

Roll out each dough portion on a lightly floured surface to a 6 inch (15 cm) circle. Spoon 1/4 cup (60 mL) beef mixture in centre of each circle, leaving a 1/2 inch (12 mm) edge. Brush edges of dough with water. Fold dough over filling. Pinch or press edges with a fork to seal. Arrange on a greased sheet of heavy duty (or double layer of regular) foil on a baking sheet. Cover with greased waxed paper and a tea towel. Let stand in oven with light on and door closed for about 30 minutes until doubled in size. Preheat barbecue to medium. Transfer empanadas on foil onto an ungreased grill. Close lid. Cook for about 10 minutes per side until empanadas are golden brown. Makes 12 empanadas.

Mexican Salad Boats

This recipe is a real crowd favourite. Romaine lettuce cradles a mixture of black beans, peppers, corn and tomatoes, turning a salad into a finger food—perfect for guests who want to mingle. Using romaine heart leaves makes these boats easier to pick up, but you may want to put a large serving spoon nearby for guests to use.

Ingredient	Imperial	Metric
Can of black beans, rinsed and drained (19 oz., 540 mL)	**1**	**1**
Can of kernel corn, drained (12 oz., 341 mL)	**1**	**1**
Chopped tomato	**1 cup**	**250 mL**
Chopped red onion	**1/2 cup**	**125 mL**
Chopped green pepper	**1/2 cup**	**125 mL**
Roasted red peppers, drained, blotted dry, chopped	**1/2 cup**	**125 mL**
Olive oil	**2 tbsp.**	**30 mL**
Lime juice	**1 tbsp.**	**15 mL**
Ground cumin	**1/2 tsp.**	**2 mL**
Chili powder	**1/2 tsp.**	**2 mL**
Pepper	**1/4 tsp.**	**1 mL**
Romaine heart leaves	**20**	**20**

Put first 6 ingredients into a medium bowl. Toss to combine.

Combine next 5 ingredients in a small bowl. Drizzle over bean mixture. Toss well to coat.

Arrange lettuce leaves on a large serving platter. Spoon bean mixture into each leaf. Makes 20 salad boats.

Chocolate Avocado Cupcakes

Chocolate cupcakes get a Mexican twist thanks to the addition of cinnamon and cayenne, as well as the unique green avocado-lime icing.

All-purpose flour	**1 1/2 cups**	**375 mL**
Granulated sugar	**1 cup**	**250 mL**
Cocoa, sifted if lumpy	**1/2 cup**	**125 mL**
Baking powder	**1 tsp.**	**5 mL**
Baking soda	**1 tsp.**	**5 mL**
Ground cinnamon	**1/2 tsp.**	**2 mL**
Cayenne pepper	**1/4 tsp.**	**1 mL**
Salt	**1/4 tsp.**	**1 mL**
Hot strong prepared coffee	**1 cup**	**250 mL**
Butter (or hard margarine), melted	**1/2 cup**	**125 mL**
Large eggs, fork-beaten	**2**	**2**
Medium ripe avocado	**1**	**1**
Icing (confectioner's) sugar	**2 1/2 cups**	**625 mL**
Lime juice	**2 tsp.**	**10 mL**
Grated lime zest	**1/2 tsp.**	**2 mL**

Combine first 8 ingredients in a large bowl. Make a well in centre.

Add coffee and butter to well. Stir until just combined. Add eggs and beat until smooth. Fill 15 greased muffin cups 3/4 full. Bake in 350°F (175°C) oven for about 20 minutes until wooden pick inserted in centre comes out clean. Let stand in pan for 10 minutes before removing to wire racks to cool completely.

For the icing, beat avocado in a medium bowl until almost smooth. Add icing sugar and beat until smooth. Add lime juice and zest. Beat until creamy. Spread over cupcakes. Makes 15 cupcakes.

Asparagus Quiche

Show Mom how much she means to you with this rich, impressive quiche. The arrival of spring means garden-fresh asparagus, which pairs beautifully with bacon and Swiss cheese to create one of the tastiest quiches you will ever experience. The perfect centerpiece for a Mother's Day brunch!

Fresh asparagus spears, trimmed of tough ends and halved	**1 lb.**	**454 g**
Salt	**1/2 tsp.**	**2 mL**
Bacon slices, diced	**8**	**8**
Grated Swiss cheese (or your favorite)	**1 cup**	**250 mL**
Unbaked 9 inch (23 cm) pie shell	**1**	**1**
Large eggs	**4**	**4**
Milk	**3/4 cup**	**175 mL**
Skim evaporated milk	**3/4 cup**	**175 mL**
Ground nutmeg	**1/8 tsp.**	**0.5 mL**
Salt	**1/2 tsp.**	**2 mL**
Pepper	**1/8 tsp.**	**0.5 mL**

Cook asparagus in water and first amount of salt in a large saucepan until tender. Drain and set aside to cool. Chop.

Fry bacon in a frying pan until golden. Drain and set aside to cool.

Scatter cheese over bottom of pie shell. Lay asparagus over cheese in spiral pattern. Scatter bacon over top.

Beat eggs in a medium bowl until frothy. Add both milks, nutmeg, second amount of salt and pepper. Beat on low until well blended. Pour over asparagus mixture. Bake on bottom rack in 350°F (175°C) oven for about 70 minutes until knife inserted in center comes out clean. Let stand for 10 minutes before cutting. Cuts into 6 wedges.

Potluck suggestion: Can serve up to 12.

Smoked Salmon Croissants

These croissants are dressed to impress! Stuffed with arugula, goat cheese, avocado, alfalfa sprouts and smoked salmon, they're a great choice for your Mother's Day luncheon.

Chopped arugula	**1/2 cup**	**125 mL**
Soft goat (chèvre) cheese	**1/2 cup**	**125 mL**
Finely chopped red onion	**2 tbsp.**	**30 mL**
Lemon juice	**1 tbsp.**	**15 mL**
Pepper	**1/8 tsp.**	**0.5 mL**
Large croissants, split	**4**	**4**
Thin slices of smoked salmon	**5 oz.**	**140 g**
Alfalfa sprouts, lightly packed	**1 cup**	**250 mL**
Thin avocado slices	**16**	**16**

Combine first 5 ingredients in a small bowl. Spread on bottom half of each croissant.

Layer remaining 3 ingredients, in order given, over cheese mixture. Cover with top halves. Makes 4 croissants.

Potluck suggestion: Cut each croissant in half to serve up to 8.

Celebrate Mom (and all the important women in your life) by throwing a garden party— even if it has to be indoors. If the weather cooperates, set up a table in the backyard filled with finger foods and surround it with comfy lawn chairs and an assortment of backyard games, such as croquet and lawn darts. If the weather is less than ideal, bring the outdoors inside: decorate the room with patio lanterns and lawn furniture and fill it with fresh flowers. Might want to pass on the lawn darts, though.

Pepper and Mushroom Salad

A mix of fresh spring lettuces forms the basis of this light, attractive salad, a perfect complement to some of the heavier dishes one would expect to see at a Mother's Day brunch. You could add some garden-fresh spinach to the mix, if you'd like.

Spring mix lettuce, lightly packed	**8 cups**	**2 L**
Jar of roasted red peppers, drained and sliced (13 oz., 370 mL)	**1**	**1**
Thinly sliced fresh white mushrooms	**1 cup**	**250 mL**
Olive (or cooking) oil	**1/3 cup**	**75 mL**
Balsamic vinegar	**2 tbsp.**	**30 mL**
Chopped fresh basil	**2 tbsp.**	**30 mL**
Liquid honey	**1 tbsp.**	**15 mL**
Garlic clove, minced	**1**	**1**
Salt	**1/4 tsp.**	**1 mL**
Whole black peppercorns, cracked	**1/4 tsp.**	**1 mL**

Combine first 3 ingredients in a large bowl. Toss lightly.

Combine remaining 7 ingredients in a jar with a tight-fitting lid. Shake well. Drizzle over salad and toss to coat well. Makes 10 servings.

Potluck suggestion: Can serve up to 15.

At a potluck of buffet, it can be a challenge to keep foods that should be refrigerated at the right temperature when they will be sitting out on a serving table for a while. To keep them cool and looking fresh, place salads and cut up fruit in a bowl that is set in a larger bowl filled with ice. Drain the water and replenish the ice as it melts.

Lemon Cream Profiteroles

These dainty, golden pastry puffs are filled with lemon cream and drizzled with a crunchy toffee. Sophisticated and delicious, they are the perfect treat to make Mom feel special.

Butter (or hard margarine)	**3 tbsp.**	**45 mL**
Water	**1/2 cup**	**125 mL**
Salt	**1/8 tsp.**	**0.5 mL**
All-purpose flour	**1/2 cup**	**125 mL**
Large eggs	**2**	**2**
Whipping cream	**1/2 cup**	**125 mL**
Mascarpone cheese, room temperature	**1/2 cup**	**125 mL**
Lemon curd	**1/3 cup**	**75 mL**
Granulated sugar	**3/4 cup**	**175 mL**
Water	**1/4 cup**	**60 mL**

Heat butter, water and salt in a heavy medium saucepan on medium-high, stirring constantly, until boiling and butter is melted. Reduce heat to medium.

Add flour all at once. Stir vigorously for about 1 minute until mixture pulls away from side of saucepan to form a soft dough. Immediately remove from heat.

Add eggs, 1 at a time, beating well after each addition, until dough is smooth and glossy. Drop by rounded teaspoonfuls (about 2 tsp., 10 mL, each), about 1 inch (2.5 cm) apart, on greased baking sheets. Bake in 425°F (220°C) oven for about 15 minutes until golden and dry. Remove to wire racks to cool.

For the filling, beat whipping cream in a small bowl until soft peaks form. Add cheese and lemon curd. Beat well. Set aside to chill. Cut off tops of profiteroles. Fill each bottom with 1 tbsp. (15 mL) filling. Replace tops. Place on a wire rack set on a baking sheet lined with wax paper.

For the toffee glaze, heat sugar and water in a small saucepan on medium, stirring constantly, until sugar is dissolved. Increase heat to medium-high. Brush inside edge of saucepan with damp pastry brush to dissolve any sugar crystals. Boil, without stirring, for about 5 minutes until sugar mixture becomes a deep, golden brown. Drizzle toffee over each profiterole. Makes 24 filled profiteroles.

Spicy Chicken-stuffed Mushrooms

On game day, one-bite finger foods are the way to go, and these stuffed mushrooms are sure to be a hit. Each bite is packed with chicken and green onion, and the sambal oelek gives the mushrooms a nice kick.

Chopped cooked chicken	**1 1/2 cups**	**250 mL**
Mayonnaise	**2 tbsp.**	**30 mL**
Sliced green onion	**2 tbsp.**	**30 mL**
Chili paste (sambal oelek)	**2 tsp.**	**10 mL**
Pepper, to taste		
Large fresh whole white mushrooms, stems removed	**24**	**24**

Combine first 5 ingredients in a small bowl.

Spray mushrooms with cooking spray. Arrange in a single layer on a baking sheet with sides. Fill with chicken mixture. Bake in 425°F (220°C) oven for about 10 minutes until mushrooms are tender and filling is heated through. Makes 24 stuffed mushrooms.

Cooked foods should be kept at room temperature for no longer than two hours. Any longer and you are putting yourself and your guests at risk of food poisoning. You might consider putting only a small amount of the food out at one time and keeping the rest of the dish in an oven that is on low to keep it warm.

Mini Pork Pitas

Mini pitas are topped with pulled pork and a fresh, shredded salad for a fun, bite-size snack that is easy to eat with much less mess than a pulled pork sandwich. As you watch the game, it is probably best to keep your hands relatively free in case of any spontaneous outbursts of enthusiasm (or despair, depending how your team is doing). About half of the pork mixture will be left over, but it freezes well.

Boneless pork shoulder blade roast, trimmed of fat	**2 lbs.**	**900 g**
Can of crushed tomatoes (14 oz., 398 mL)	**1**	**1**
Balsamic vinegar	**1/4 cup**	**60 mL**
Greek seasoning	**2 tbsp.**	**30 mL**
Granulated sugar	**2 tsp.**	**10 mL**
Smoked (sweet) paprika	**1 tsp.**	**5 mL**
Pepper	**1/2 tsp.**	**2 mL**
Lemon juice	**1 tbsp.**	**15 mL**
Shredded romaine lettuce, lightly packed	**1 cup**	**250 mL**
Diced English cucumber (with peel)	**1/2 cup**	**125 mL**
Diced seeded tomato	**1/2 cup**	**125 mL**
Chopped fresh mint	**2 tbsp.**	**30 mL**
Finely chopped red onion	**2 tbsp.**	**30 mL**
Pita breads (3 inch, 7.5 cm, diameter)	**24**	**24**
Sliced red onion, for garnish		

Place roast in 3 1/2 to 4 quart (3.5 to 4 L) slow cooker.

Combine next 6 ingredients in a medium bowl. Pour over roast. Cook, covered, on High for 4 1/2 to 5 hours. Transfer roast to a large plate. Skim and discard fat from sauce. Shred pork using 2 forks. Remove and discard any fat. Return pork to slow cooker. Stir in lemon juice.

Combine next 5 ingredients in a medium bowl.

Arrange lettuce mixture over pitas. Top with pork mixture. Garnish with red onion. Makes 24 mini pitas.

Smoky Mac 'n' Cheese

This aromatic version of macaroni and cheese is comfort food at its finest. Your guests will be sure to leave room on their plate for a scoop or two.

Water	**8 cups**	**2 L**
Salt	**1 tsp.**	**5 mL**
Elbow macaroni	**2 cups**	**500 mL**
Butter (or hard margarine)	**2 tbsp.**	**30 mL**
Finely chopped onion	**1/4 cup**	**60 mL**
All-purpose flour	**2 tbsp.**	**30 mL**
Milk	**2 cups**	**500 mL**
Grated smoked Gouda cheese	**1 cup**	**250 mL**
Grated sharp Cheddar cheese	**1/2 cup**	**125 mL**
Grated Parmesan cheese	**1/4 cup**	**60 mL**
Dijon mustard	**2 tsp.**	**10 mL**
Salt	**1/2 tsp.**	**2 mL**
Cayenne pepper, to taste (optional)		
Cooked bacon slices, crumbled	**8**	**8**
Fine dry bread crumbs	**3 tbsp.**	**45 mL**
Butter (or hard margarine), melted	**1 tbsp.**	**15 mL**

Combine water and salt in a large saucepan. Bring to a boil. Add pasta. Boil, uncovered, for 8 to 10 minutes, stirring occasionally, until tender but firm. Drain. Transfer to greased 2 quart (2 L) casserole.

Melt butter in a medium saucepan on medium. Add onion and cook for about 3 minutes, stirring often, until softened.

Add flour. Heat, stirring, for 1 minute. Slowly add milk, stirring constantly until smooth. Heat, stirring, until boiling and thickened. Remove from heat.

Add next 6 ingredients. Stir until cheese is melted. Add to pasta and stir until coated. Stir in bacon.

Combine bread crumbs and melted butter in a small bowl. Sprinkle over pasta mixture. Bake, uncovered, in 350°F (175°C) oven for about 30 minutes until bubbling and golden. Makes 4 servings.

Potluck suggestion: Can serve up to 8.

Barbecued Shrimp

Victoria Day marks the beginning of barbecue season, so fire up the grill and cook up some perfectly barbecued shrimp. The garlic and lemon mayonnaise can easily be made a day or two ahead and stored in a sealed container in the refrigerator.

Garlic clove (or 1/4 tsp., 1 mL, powder)	**1**	**1**
Large egg	**1**	**1**
Egg yolk (large)	**1**	**1**
Lemon juice	**1 tbsp.**	**15 mL**
Salt	**1/8 tsp.**	**0.5 mL**
Olive (or cooking) oil	**3/4 cup**	**175 mL**
Cooking oil	**2 tbsp.**	**30 mL**
Chopped fresh parsley (or 2 1/4 tsp., 11 mL, flakes)	**3 tbsp.**	**45 mL**
Finely grated lemon zest	**1/2 tsp.**	**2 mL**
Salt	**1/2 tsp.**	**2 mL**
Coarsely ground pepper (or 1/2 tsp., 2 mL, pepper)	**1 tsp.**	**5 mL**
Jumbo shrimp (tails intact), peeled and deveined	**18**	**18**
Bamboo skewers (10 inch, 25 cm, each) soaked in water for 10 minutes	**6**	**6**

Process first 5 ingredients in a blender for about 2 minutes until well combined and creamy.

With motor running, slowly pour olive oil in a thin stream through feed chute until pale and thickened. Cover and chill for at least 1 to 2 hours or overnight.

Combine next 5 ingredients in a medium bowl.

Add shrimp, and toss until coated. Marinate, covered, in refrigerator for 1 hour, stirring occasionally. Drain and discard any remaining marinade. Preheat gas barbecue to medium. Thread shrimp onto skewers and cook on a greased grill for about 2 minutes per side until pink. Do not overcook. Serve with mayonnaise. Makes 18 shrimp.

Pork Satay

The Victoria Day long weekend also signals the beginning of camping season, and this is a great dish to take along on your camping trip or to a get-together where you will be cooking over a fire pit. You can even freeze the pork cubes in the marinade to make them easier and safer to transport to your campsite or picnic.

Frozen concentrated orange juice	**1/4 cup**	**60 mL**
Low-sodium soy sauce	**1 tbsp.**	**15 mL**
Cooking oil	**1 tbsp.**	**15 mL**
Garlic cloves, minced (or 1/2 tsp., 2 mL, powder)	**2**	**2**
Finely grated gingerroot (or 1/2 tsp., 2 mL, ground ginger)	**2 tsp.**	**10 mL**
Hot pepper sauce	**1/4 tsp.**	**1 mL**
Pork loin, cut into 1 inch (2.5 cm) cubes	**1 lb.**	**454 g**

Combine first 6 ingredients in a small bowl.

Place pork cubes in a large resealable freezer bag. Pour marinade over top. Seal and turn to coat. Marinate in refrigerator (or cooler) for at least 3 hours. Remove pork cubes and discard marinade. Push about 4 or 5 pork cubes onto each of 4 roasting sticks. Lay on top of grill over hot coals in a fire pit. Cook for 10 minutes, turning several times, until no longer pink inside. Makes 4 servings.

Potluck suggestion: Can serve up to 8.

When transporting meat in a cooler, pack it at the bottom, where the temperatures are coldest, and where there is less risk of cross-contamination should the container or bag the meat is in leak. You really don't want raw meat juices coming into contact with the other foods in your cooler.

Greek Rotini Salad

This salad has all the fresh veggies, tangy olives and feta of a classic Greek salad, but is more substantial thanks to the addition of pasta. A great vegetarian option for a Victoria Day barbecue. You could pack the dressing separately and add it to the pasta once you arrive at your event.

Cooked rotini pasta (about 1 1/2 cups, 375 mL, uncooked)	**3 cups**	**750 mL**
Diced English cucumber (with peel)	**1 cup**	**250 mL**
Grape tomatoes, halved	**20**	**20**
Chopped green pepper	**1/2 cup**	**125 mL**
Chopped red onion	**1/2 cup**	**125 mL**
Chopped red pepper	**1/2 cup**	**125 mL**
Whole pitted kalamata olives	**1/4 cup**	**60 mL**
Olive oil	**1/3 cup**	**75 mL**
Lemon juice	**3 tbsp.**	**45 mL**
Chopped fresh parsley (or 1 1/2 tsp., 7 mL, flakes)	**2 tbsp.**	**30 mL**
Chopped fresh oregano (or 1/4 tsp., 1 mL, dried)	**1 tsp.**	**5 mL**
Garlic clove, minced (or 1/4 tsp., 1 mL, powder)	**1**	**1**
Salt	**1/4 tsp.**	**1 mL**
Pepper	**1/8 tsp.**	**0.5 mL**
Crumbled feta cheese	**3/4 cup**	**175 mL**

Combine first 7 ingredients in a large bowl.

Combine next 7 ingredients in a jar with a tight-fitting lid. Shake well. Drizzle over pasta mixture. Toss to coat.

Sprinkle with cheese. Makes about 6 cups (1.5 L).

Potluck suggestion: Can serve up to 12.

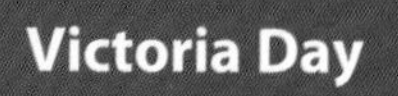

Crispy Chicken

Whether you are celebrating Father's Day with a get-together at home or a picnic in the park, this dish will be a huge hit. The thyme-flavoured coating gives the chicken real crunch.

All-purpose flour	**3/4 cup**	**175 mL**
Paprika	**1 tsp.**	**5 mL**
Ground thyme	**1 tsp.**	**5 mL**
Salt	**1 tsp.**	**5 mL**
Pepper	**1/4 tsp.**	**1 mL**
Large egg	**1**	**1**
Milk	**2 tbsp.**	**30 mL**
Lemon juice	**2 tsp.**	**10 mL**
Bone-in chicken parts	**3 lbs.**	**1.4 kg**
Butter (or hard margarine), melted	**1/4 cup**	**60 mL**

Combine first 5 ingredients in a shallow dish.

Beat egg in a separate shallow dish. Stir in milk and lemon juice.

Dip chicken into flour mixture, then into egg mixture. Dip back into flour mixture until coated. Arrange chicken, skin side up, in a single layer on greased baking sheet. Let stand for 30 minutes.

Drizzle with butter. Bake in 350°F (175°C) oven for 1 to 1 1/4 hours until tender. Makes 6 servings.

Potluck suggestion: Can serve up to 12.

If you are transporting the chicken (or any other hot dish) to a picnic site, keep it warm by packing it in an insulated container, or wrap it in foil and then with heavy towels or layers of newspaper.

Grilled Steak and Vegetables

Treat Dad right with crisp, fresh vegetables and deliciously barbecued steak—summer dining at its best! You might have to cook the vegetables in two batches.

Fresh whole white mushrooms	**18**	**18**
Medium zucchini (with peel), cut into 1/2 inch (12 mm) thick slices	**2**	**2**
Medium red onion, cut into wedges	**1**	**1**
Medium red pepper, cut into wedges, seeds and ribs removed	**1**	**1**
Medium yellow pepper, cut into wedges, seeds and ribs removed	**1**	**1**
Low-fat Italian dressing	**3/4 cup**	**175 mL**
Brown sugar, packed	**2 tbsp.**	**30 mL**
Olive (or cooking) oil	**1 tbsp.**	**15 mL**
Dry mustard	**1 tsp.**	**5 mL**
Ground coriander	**1 tsp.**	**5 mL**
Garlic cloves, minced (or 3/4 tsp., 4 mL, powder)	**3**	**3**
Salt	**1 tsp.**	**5 mL**
Pepper	**2 tsp.**	**10 mL**
Top sirloin, flank or inside round steak	**2 lbs.**	**900 g**

Put first 5 ingredients into a large bowl. Stir in dressing until evenly coated. Cover with plastic wrap and marinate in refrigerator for 2 to 3 hours, stirring occasionally. Drain and discard liquid from vegetables. Spread vegetable mixture evenly in a large greased foil pan. Preheat barbecue to medium. Place pan on an ungreased grill. Cook vegetables for 8 to 10 minutes, stirring occasionally, until tender-crisp. Remove from heat and cover with foil to keep warm.

Combine next 7 ingredients in a small bowl. Spread over both sides of steak. Reduce heat to medium-low. Cook steak on a greased grill for 7 to 10 minutes per side until desired doneness. Cut diagonally into 1/4 inch (6 mm) thick slices. Serve with vegetables. Makes 8 servings.

Bean and Cashew Salad

Dress up the dinner table for Father's Day with this unique, colourful salad combination. Fresh green beans make this salad truly spectacular. Walnuts would work well in place of the cashews, if you prefer.

Fresh whole green beans	**1/2 lb.**	**225 g**
Halved cherry tomatoes	**2 cups**	**500 mL**
Plain cashews, toasted	**1 cup**	**250 mL**
Thinly sliced red onion	**3/4 cup**	**175 mL**
Olive (or cooking) oil	**1/3 cup**	**75 mL**
Lemon juice	**3 tbsp.**	**45 mL**
Chopped fresh dill (or 1/2 tsp., 2 mL, dill weed)	**2 tsp.**	**10 mL**
Garlic clove, minced (or 1/4 tsp., 1 mL, powder)	**1**	**1**
Chili paste (sambal oelek)	**1/2 tsp.**	**2 mL**
Salt	**1/4 tsp.**	**1 mL**

Blanch beans in boiling water in a large saucepan for 1 to 3 minutes until bright green. Drain and immediately plunge into ice water in a large bowl. Let stand for about 10 minutes until cold. Drain and transfer to a separate large bowl.

Add tomato, cashews and onion and toss lightly.

Combine remaining 6 ingredients in a jar with a tight-fitting lid. Shake well. Drizzle over salad and toss well. Makes 8 servings.

Cooking times will vary when toasting different types of nuts, seeds or coconut, so never toast them together. For small amounts, place the ingredient in an ungreased frying pan and heat on medium for 3 to 5 minutes, stirring often, until golden. For larger amounts, spread the ingredient evenly in an ungreased shallow pan and bake in a 350°F (175°C) oven for 5 to 10 minutes, stirring or shaking often, until golden.

Cedar Plank Salmon

Canadian whisky, maple syrup and salmon—what could be more Canadian? This is the perfect meal to celebrate Canada's birthday. The delicately sweet maple syrup perfectly complements the light smoky flavour of the salmon.

Cedar planks	**2**	**2**
Canadian whisky (rye)	**1 cup**	**250 mL**
Maple syrup	**1/2 cup**	**125 mL**
Soy sauce	**1/3 cup**	**75 mL**
Olive (or cooking) oil	**1/4 cup**	**60 mL**
Parsley flakes	**1/4 cup**	**60 mL**
Sweet (or regular) chili sauce	**3 tbsp.**	**45 mL**
Pepper	**1 tsp.**	**5 mL**
Salmon fillets (about 4 oz., 113 g, each), or side of salmon (about 2 lbs., 900 g), skin removed, cut into 8 equal pieces	**8**	**8**

Place cedar planks in a large container and add enough water to cover. Weight planks with heavy cans to keep them submerged. Let stand for at least 6 hours or overnight to soak.

Combine whisky and next 6 ingredients in a medium bowl.

Place salmon in a large, shallow baking dish. Pour marinade over top. Turn until coated. Cover and marinate in refrigerator for at least 30 minutes, turning occasionally. Drain and discard marinade. Preheat barbecue to medium-low and place salmon on cedar planks on an ungreased grill. Close lid and cook for 15 to 30 minutes until salmon flakes easily when tested with a fork. Makes 8 servings.

Cedar planks specifically designed for barbecuing can be purchased in the meat department of large grocery stores. Or use an untreated western red cedar plank found in building supply stores. Never use a treated cedar plank. Planks should be about 16 x 6 x 1/2 inches (40 x 15 x 1.2 cm) and are good for 1 use each.

Spinach Wild Rice Salad

Wild rice grows in the shallow water of small lakes and wetlands in Canada's boreal forest and has been a staple for Indigenous peoples for thousands of years. Celebrate Canada's heritage with this wild rice salad that also features Canada's national apple, the McIntosh.

Cooked long-grain and wild rice mix, (about 2/3 cup, 150 mL, uncooked)	**2 cups**	**500 mL**
Sliced fresh white mushrooms	**2 cups**	**500 mL**
Cooked hard red wheat	**1 cup**	**250 mL**
Diced unpeeled McIntosh apple	**1 cup**	**250 mL**
Chopped pecans, toasted (see sidebar, page 70)	**1/2 cup**	**125 mL**
Diced yellow pepper	**1/2 cup**	**125 mL**
Apple cider vinegar	**1/4 cup**	**60 mL**
Cooking oil	**1/4 cup**	**60 mL**
Frozen concentrated apple juice, thawed	**1/4 cup**	**60 mL**
Garlic clove, minced (or 1/4 tsp., 1 mL, powder)	**1**	**1**
Ground cinnamon	**1/4 tsp.**	**1 mL**
Ground nutmeg	**1/4 tsp.**	**1 mL**
Salt	**1/4 tsp.**	**1 mL**
Pepper	**1/4 tsp.**	**1 mL**
Fresh spinach leaves, lightly packed	**3 cups**	**750 mL**

Combine first 6 ingredients in a large bowl.

Combine next 8 ingredients in a jar with a tight-fitting lid. Shake well. Drizzle over rice mixture. Toss until coated.

Add spinach and toss lightly. Makes about 9 1/2 cups (2.4 L).

Potluck suggestion: Can serve up to 12.

To prepare the hard red wheat (also called wheat berries), soak 1/2 cup (125 mL) overnight. To cook the wheat, bring 1 1/4 cups (300 mL) water and a pinch of salt to a boil in a small saucepan. Add the drained wheat and simmer, covered, on medium-low for about 1 3/4 hours until the liquid is absorbed and the wheat is tender. Makes about 1 1/4 cups (300 mL). Extra wheat can be frozen in an airtight container.

Maple Bacon Sundae

Top off your Canada Day celebration with this delicious sundae. Maple syrup. Bacon. Ice cream. Enough said.

Maple syrup	**1 cup**	**250 mL**
Cooked, crispy double-smoked bacon, crumbled	**1/2 cup**	**125 mL**
Chopped pecans	**1/2 cup**	**125 mL**
Vanilla ice cream	**8 cups**	**2 L**

Heat syrup in a saucepan over medium. Bring to a boil and cook until slightly reduced. Stir in bacon. Stir in nuts and remove from heat. Let stand for a few minutes.

Divide ice cream among 6 bowls. Top with sauce and serve. Makes 6 servings.

Potluck suggestion: Can serve up to 12.

Fruit Pizza

With the summer heat comes the arrival of a wide variety of much anticipated, locally grown fresh fruit, just bursting with flavour, and this dessert is the perfect way to show it off. To make this dessert the ultimate Canada Day treat, arrange the fruit in the shape of the Canadian flag.

All-purpose flour	**1 1/4 cups**	**300 mL**
Brown sugar, packed	**1/3 cup**	**75 mL**
Icing (confectioner's) sugar	**3 tbsp.**	**45 mL**
Butter (or hard margarine), cut up	**2/3 cup**	**150 mL**
Blocks of cream cheese (4 oz., 125 g, each), softened	**3**	**3**
Granulated sugar	**1/2 cup**	**125 mL**
Vanilla	**1 tsp.**	**5 mL**
Variety of fresh fruit (such as strawberries, kiwifruit, peaches or raspberries), sliced		
Apricot jam (or orange marmalade)	**1/4 cup**	**60 mL**
Water	**1 tbsp.**	**15 mL**

Combine flour, brown sugar and icing sugar in a medium bowl. Cut in butter until mixture resembles fine crumbs. Press mixture together to form a smooth ball. Press firmly in ungreased 12 inch (30 cm) pizza pan. Bake in 350°F (175°C) oven for 10 to 15 minutes until golden. Let stand in pan on a wire rack until cooled completely.

For the topping, beat cream cheese, sugar and vanilla in a large bowl until smooth. Spread evenly over crust. Arrange fruit in an attractive pattern over cream cheese mixture.

For the glaze, combine apricot jam and water in a small bowl. Press through sieve into a separate small bowl. Brush lightly over fruit. Chill. Cuts into 12 wedges.

Potluck suggestion: Can cut into up to 18 pieces.

Spicy Threaded Beef

A Fourth of July celebration would not be complete without a little beef on the barbie, and these delicious skewers make a nice change from the usual burgers or steak. The secret to great beef skewers is to marinate the meat properly, preferably overnight, and make sure you do not overcook them. The beef strips will continue to cook a little after they come off the grill, so adjust your cooking time accordingly.

Flank steak	**1 1/2 lbs.**	**680 g**
Low-sodium soy sauce	**1/4 cup**	**60 mL**
Tequila	**1/4 cup**	**60 mL**
Freshly squeezed juice of 2 limes		
Small hot chilies, seeds removed and chopped fine (see sidebar, page 150)	**3**	**3**
Garlic cloves, minced	**4**	**4**
Finely grated gingerroot	**1 tbsp.**	**15 mL**
Canola oil	**1 tbsp.**	**15 mL**
Bamboo skewers (10 inch, 25 cm, each), soaked in water for 10 minutes	**12**	**12**
Prepared orange juice	**1/2 cup**	**125 mL**
Brown sugar, packed	**1 tbsp.**	**15 mL**
Cornstarch	**2 tsp.**	**10 mL**

Cut steak on diagonal across grain into 1/2 inch (12 mm) thick slices. Place in a sealable plastic bag.

Combine next 7 ingredients in a small bowl. Pour over beef strips and seal bag. Marinate in refrigerator for several hours or overnight, turning several times. Drain and reserve marinade. Push beef strips onto skewers, accordion style.

Strain remaining marinade through a sieve and discard solids. Combine orange juice with strained marinade in a small saucepan. Combine brown sugar and cornstarch in a small cup. Stir into mixture in saucepan. Bring to a boil, stirring until thickened. Preheat barbecue to medium-high. Place skewers on a lightly greased grill. Cook for about 3 minutes per side, basting occasionally with thickened sauce, until desired doneness. Reheat remaining sauce to boiling before serving. Makes 12 skewers.

 The steak will be easier to slice if it is partially frozen.

Pecan Tart

Celebrate Independence Day with this rich, sweet tart that is loaded with pecans. The perfect treat for Fourth of July festivities.

Pastry for 9 inch (23 cm) pie shell	**1**	**1**
Large eggs	**4**	**4**
Brown sugar, packed	**1 cup**	**250 mL**
Golden corn syrup	**2/3 cup**	**150 mL**
Butter (or hard margarine), melted	**1/4 cup**	**60 mL**
Vanilla	**1 tsp.**	**5 mL**
Finely grated orange zest	**1 tsp.**	**5 mL**
Salt	**1/4 tsp.**	**1 mL**
Chopped pecans, toasted (see sidebar, page 70)	**2 cups**	**500 mL**
Pecan halves	**16**	**16**

Roll out pastry on a lightly floured surface to about 1/8 inch (3 mm) thickness. Press in bottom and up side of a 9 inch (23 cm) tart pan with fluted side and a removable bottom. Trim edge. Cover and chill for 30 minutes.

Beat eggs in a large bowl until frothy. Add next 6 ingredients. Beat well.

Place tart pan on a baking sheet (to make it easier to remove hot pan from oven). Sprinkle chopped pecans over pastry. Pour egg mixture over pecans.

Arrange pecan halves around edge of filling. Bake on bottom rack in 400°F (200°C) oven for 10 minutes. Reduce heat to 350°F (175°C). Bake for about 35 minutes until filling is set and pastry is golden brown. Let stand in pan on wire rack to cool completely. Cuts into 8 wedges.

Potluck suggestion: Can serve up to 12.

Caponata

At your next summer picnic, take advantage of summer's bounty with our version of caponata, loaded with fresh peppers, zucchini and eggplant. Traditionally a classic Sicilian stew, caponata is incredibly versatile and can be served over rice or pasta, as a topping on grilled meats or seafood or as an appetizer served with bread or crackers. For this recipe, we've gone the appetizer route. It is best served chilled or at room temperature with whole-grain crackers or pita bread.

Ingredient	Imperial	Metric
Chopped peeled eggplant (1 1/2 inch, 4 cm, pieces)	**5 cups**	**1.25 L**
Olive oil	**1 tbsp.**	**15 mL**
Chopped onion	**1 cup**	**250 mL**
Finely chopped celery	**1 cup**	**250 mL**
Garlic cloves, minced	**2**	**2**
Dried crushed chilies	**1/4 tsp.**	**1 mL**
Can of diced tomatoes (with juice) (14 oz., 398 mL)	**1**	**1**
Diced red pepper	**1 cup**	**250 mL**
Diced zucchini (with peel)	**1 cup**	**250 mL**
Balsamic vinegar	**2 tbsp.**	**30 mL**
Tomato paste	**1 tbsp.**	**15 mL**
Granulated sugar	**2 tsp.**	**10 mL**
Dried oregano	**1 1/2 tsp.**	**7 mL**
Chopped olives	**1/3 cup**	**75 mL**
Chopped capers (optional)	**2 tsp.**	**10 mL**
Chopped fresh basil	**1 tbsp.**	**15 mL**
Chopped pine nuts, toasted (see sidebar, page 70)	**1 tbsp.**	**15 mL**

Arrange eggplant in a single layer on a greased baking sheet. Broil on top rack in oven for about 5 minutes, stirring occasionally, until browned and starting to soften. Transfer to greased 3 1/2 to 4 quart (3.5 to 4 L) slow cooker.

Heat olive oil in a large frying pan on medium. Add onion and celery. Cook for about 8 minutes, stirring often, until onion starts to soften. Add garlic and chilies. Heat, stirring, for about 1 minute until fragrant. Add to slow cooker.

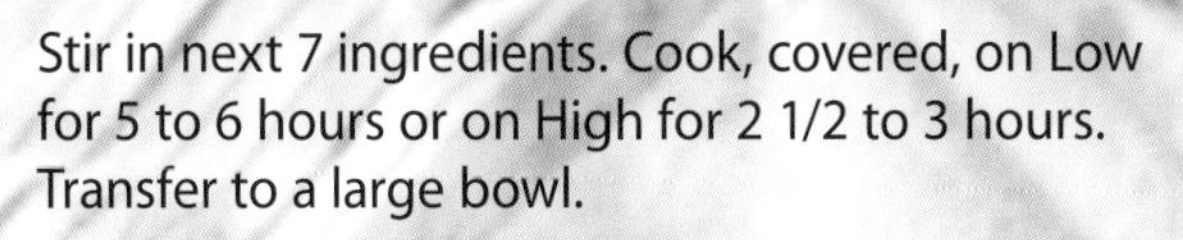

Stir in next 7 ingredients. Cook, covered, on Low for 5 to 6 hours or on High for 2 1/2 to 3 hours. Transfer to a large bowl.

Stir in olives and capers. Chill, covered, for at least 6 hours.

Sprinkle with basil and pine nuts. Makes about 4 1/2 cups (1.1 L).

Potluck suggestion: Can serve up to 10.

Buffalo Beer Ribs

Take ribs, a classic chicken wing sauce and a couple of cans of beer and you get a tender show-stopper with a spicy bite! This makes a perfect dish for a summer picnic. Just make sure you pack plenty of napkins or wet wipes!

Pork side ribs, trimmed of fat and cut into 3-bone portions	**4 lbs.**	**1.8 kg**
Cans of beer (12 1/2 oz., 355 mL, each)	**2**	**2**
Butter (or hard margarine)	**1/4 cup**	**60 mL**
Garlic cloves, minced (or 1/2 tsp., 2 mL, powder)	**2**	**2**
Can of tomato sauce (7 1/2 oz., 213 mL)	**1**	**1**
Brown sugar, packed	**1/4 cup**	**60 mL**
Louisiana hot sauce	**3 tbsp.**	**45 mL**
Apple cider vinegar	**1 tbsp.**	**15 mL**
Dried oregano	**2 tsp.**	**10 mL**
Salt	**1/2 tsp.**	**2 mL**
Pepper	**1/2 tsp.**	**2 mL**

Place ribs in a Dutch oven or large pot. Pour beer over top and add water to cover. Bring to a boil. Reduce heat to medium-low and simmer, covered, for about 1 hour until ribs are tender. Drain.

Melt butter in a medium saucepan on medium. Add garlic and cook for about 5 minutes, stirring often, until fragrant.

Add remaining 7 ingredients and bring to a boil. Reduce heat to low and simmer for 10 minutes to blend flavours. Let stand for about 10 minutes until slightly cooled. Preheat gas barbecue to medium. Place ribs on greased grill. Close lid and cook for about 15 minutes, turning twice and brushing with tomato mixture until ribs are glazed and heated through. Makes 10 servings.

Teriyaki Turkey Skewers

These skewers are great picnic fare. To make things easier at the picnic site, thread the meat and veggies onto the skewers at home and store them in a foil pan with a lid. Transport the sauce in a container or jar with a tight-fitting lid to prevent any spills.

Ingredient	Imperial	Metric
Teriyaki sauce	**1/2 cup**	**125 mL**
Liquid honey	**2 tbsp.**	**30 mL**
Ketchup	**2 tbsp.**	**30 mL**
Pepper	**1 tsp.**	**5 mL**
Garlic powder	**1/2 tsp.**	**2 mL**
Ground ginger	**1/2 tsp.**	**2 mL**
Cayenne pepper	**1/4 tsp.**	**1 mL**
Boneless, skinless turkey breast half, cut into 1 inch (2.5 cm) cubes	**1 1/2 lbs.**	**680 g**
Fresh pineapple, cut into 3/4 inch (2 cm) pieces	**2 1/2 cups**	**625 mL**
Medium green pepper, seeds and ribs removed, cut into 3/4 inch (2 cm) pieces	**2 1/2 cups**	**625 mL**
Bamboo skewers (12 inch, 30 cm, length), soaked in water for 10 minutes	**12**	**12**

Combine first 7 ingredients in a small bowl. Set aside.

Thread turkey, pineapple and green pepper alternately onto skewers. Preheat barbecue to medium. Cook skewers on a greased grill for 12 to 15 minutes, turning occasionally and brushing with sauce, until turkey is no longer pink inside. Makes 12 skewers.

Mexican Sliders

To take these cute mini burgers along on your next picnic, make sure you pack the patties separately from the salsa mixture and lettuce, and assemble them right before you serve them. If you have access to a barbecue or fire pit at the picnic site, all the better. Make the patties at home, wrap them in plastic wrap, and pack them into the cooler, under the cheese slices and lettuce. Cook them for about 5 minutes per side once you arrive at the picnic. They will be even tastier fresh off the grill!

Chopped cilantro (or fresh parsley)	**3 tbsp.**	**45 mL**
Fine dry bread crumbs	**2 tbsp.**	**30 mL**
Dried oregano	**1/2 tsp.**	**2 mL**
Ground cumin	**1/2 tsp.**	**2 mL**
Ground coriander	**1/4 tsp.**	**1 mL**
Salt	**1/4 tsp.**	**1 mL**
Garlic clove, minced (or 1/4 tsp., 1 mL, powder)	**1**	**1**
Extra-lean ground beef	**12 oz.**	**340 g**
Uncooked chorizo (or hot Italian) sausage, casing removed	**4 oz.**	**113 g**
Small slices of Monterey Jack cheese	**12**	**12**
Canned refried beans	**2/3 cup**	**150 mL**
Salsa	**1/4 cup**	**60 mL**
Small cocktail or slider buns, halved	**12**	**12**
Shredded Romaine lettuce	**1 cup**	**250 mL**

Combine first 7 ingredients in a bowl. Add beef and sausage. Mix well. Form 12 patties, each about 1/2 inch (12 mm) thick. Place on a greased baking sheet with sides. Bake in 400°F (200°C) oven for 8 minutes until internal temperature reaches 160°F (71°C).

Top patties with cheese. Bake for about 2 minutes until cheese is melted.

Combine refried beans and salsa in a small bowl. Spread on bottom halves of buns. Top with lettuce. Place patties on lettuce. Makes 12 sliders.

If you don't use the full can of refried beans, you can keep the remainder for a day or two in the fridge. The beans also freeze well, so portion them in 1/4 to 1/3 cup (60 to 75 mL) amounts and freeze for later use.

Watermelon and Feta Salad

The expression "the whole is greater than the sum of its parts" could have been coined for this fantastic recipe. This fun, cool salad is so much more flavourful than you'd expect from the simplicity of the ingredients and the ease of preparation. Transport the salad, basil oil and balsamic dressing to your picnic separately, and add the basil oil and dressing just before serving.

Balsamic vinegar	**1 cup**	**250 mL**
Basil leaves	**1 cup**	**250 mL**
Olive oil	**3 tbsp.**	**45 mL**
Large seedless watermelon	**1/2**	**1/2**
Feta cheese	**10 oz.**	**285 g**
Frisée, trimmed and cut into large pieces	**1 cup**	**250 mL**

Heat balsamic vinegar in a small heavy bottomed pot on high until reduced by half. Set aside to cool.

Add basil to a small blender. With motor running, slowly add oil until combined.

Cut watermelon vertically into 3/4 inch (2 cm) slices. Remove peel and cut flesh roughly into 2 inch (5 cm) triangles. Set aside.

Cut feta into 1/2 inch (12 mm) slices and cut roughly into 1 inch (2.5 cm) triangles. Lay watermelon and feta on a large plate in a repeating sequence, i.e. watermelon, then feta, then watermelon and so on.

Transfer vinegar reduction to a small resealable bag (or fine-tipped piping bag). Poke a tiny hole in bottom corner of resealable bag and drizzle vinegar reduction over top of watermelon and feta. Spoon drops of basil oil over top. Garnish with frisée. Serve chilled. Makes 6 servings.

Potluck suggestion: Can serve up to 12.

Chipotle-braised Short Ribs

Short ribs are meaty, beefy ribs. They need a long, slow cooking time, and they are not typically cooked on the grill. In this recipe, though, the ribs are dusted with a dry rub and then slow-cooked over indirect heat for 3 to 4 hours, until the meat falls off the bone. Start the cooking process before your guests arrive, and they will be drawn to your yard by the delicious aroma. Because these short ribs are so rich, you don't need many to make a great meal.

Dried oregano	**3 tbsp.**	**45 mL**
Dried parsley flakes	**2 tsp.**	**10 mL**
Dried thyme leaves	**2 tbsp.**	**30 mL**
Kosher salt	**2 tbsp.**	**30 mL**
Cracked black pepper	**1 tbsp.**	**15 mL**
Ground chipotle powder	**2 tsp.**	**10 mL**
Garlic powder	**1 tsp.**	**5 mL**
Brown sugar	**1 tbsp.**	**15 mL**
Barbecue sauce	**1/2 cup**	**125 mL**
Beer	**1/2 cup**	**125 mL**
Beef short ribs, trimmed of almost all fat	**3 lbs.**	**1.4 kg**

Preheat one side of barbecue to low and leave the other side off. Combine first 8 ingredients in a small bowl or resealable freezer bag.

Combine next two ingredients in a small bowl.

In small batches, dredge short ribs in rub and place on off side of barbecue. Close lid and cook for 3 hours, checking about every 45 minutes, flipping meat and brushing it with beer mixture. When ribs are done—when meat is falling off bones—brush again with beer mixture. Remove from heat and serve. Makes 6 servings.

Potluck suggestion: Can serve up to 12.

Lime Chicken and Salsa

These chicken breasts are simple to prepare and quick to the table, but make sure you allow enough time for the chicken to marinate in its sweet and spicy sauce. The grilled salsa really sets this dish apart.

Sweet (or regular) chili sauce	1/4 cup	60 mL
Peanut (or cooking) oil	2 tbsp.	30 mL
Lime juice	1/4 cup	60 mL
Finely grated lime zest	1 tsp.	5 mL
Fish sauce	2 tsp.	10 mL
Brown sugar, packed	2 tsp.	10 mL
Finely grated gingerroot (or 1/4 tsp., 1 mL, ground ginger)	2 tsp.	10 mL
Garlic cloves, minced (or 1/4 tsp., 1 mL, powder)	2	2
Salt	1/2 tsp.	2 mL
Boneless, skinless chicken breast halves (about 1 lb., 454 g)	8	8
Small red pepper, quartered	2	2
Cans of pineapple slices (14 oz., 398 mL), drained and 1 tbsp. (15 mL) juice reserved	2	2
Small zucchini, with peel, cut lengthwise into 1/4 inch (6 mm) thick slices	2	2
Lime juice	2 tbsp.	30 mL
Reserved pineapple juice	2 tbsp.	30 mL
Peanut (or cooking) oil	2 tbsp.	30 mL
Chopped salted peanuts	6 tbsp.	90 mL
Garlic cloves, minced (or 1/4 tsp., 1 mL, powder)	2	2
Salt	1/2 tsp.	2 mL

Combine first 9 ingredients in a large bowl or resealable freezer bag.

Add chicken and turn to coat. Cover or seal. Marinate in refrigerator for 2 hours. Drain and discard marinade. Preheat electric grill for 5 minutes or gas barbecue to medium. Cook chicken on a greased grill for about 5 minutes per side until no longer pink inside.

For the salsa, place red pepper, pineapple and zucchini on greased grill. Cook for 5 to 7 minutes, turning once, until grill marks appear and pepper and zucchini are tender-crisp. Finely chop pepper, pineapple and zucchini. Put into a medium bowl.

Stir in remaining 6 ingredients. Serve with chicken. Makes 8 servings.

Tomato Salad with Orange Basil Dressing

This colourful combination of contrasting textures and tastes is accented with a slightly sweet and tangy dressing. It is the perfect complement to any grilled meat dish.

Halved cherry tomatoes	**2 cups**	**500 mL**
Chopped English cucumber (with peel)	**1 cup**	**250 mL**
Frozen (or canned) kernel corn, thawed	**1 cup**	**250 mL**
Frozen concentrated orange juice	**2 tbsp.**	**30 mL**
Chopped fresh basil (or 3/4 tsp. 4 mL, dried)	**1 tbsp.**	**15 mL**
Olive oil	**1 tbsp.**	**15 mL**
Apple cider vinegar	**2 tsp.**	**10 mL**
Dijon mustard	**1 tsp.**	**5 mL**
Grated orange zest	**1/2 tsp.**	**2 mL**
Liquid honey	**1/2 tsp.**	**2 mL**
Salt	**1/4 tsp.**	**1 mL**
Pepper	**1/8 tsp.**	**0.5 mL**

Combine first 3 ingredients in a medium bowl.

For the dressing, combine next 9 ingredients in a small jar with a tight-fitting lid. Shake well. Drizzle over tomato mixture and toss to coat. Let stand for 30 minutes, stirring occasionally. Makes about 4 cups (1 L).

Potluck suggestion: Can serve up to 8.

To prevent a traffic jam of hungry guests at your backyard barbecue, consider setting up two different tables, one for the mains and sides, and another for the beverages and desserts. Plates and utensils can be set up on the table with the mains, and cups or glasses can go on the beverage and desserts table.

Citrus Shrimp Salad Ceviche

This fresh mixture of peppers, shrimp, tomato and avocado is reminiscent of the kind of food you would get in the coastal regions of Latin America—certainly a treat and certainly tantalizing! Treat your guests to a culinary journey in the comfort of your own backyard. If you like, substitute minced chipotle pepper for the chili powder. Serve with tortilla chips.

Uncooked medium shrimp (peeled and deveined)	**1 lb.**	**454 g**
Finely chopped green pepper	**1/4 cup**	**60 mL**
Finely chopped orange (or red) pepper	**1/4 cup**	**60 mL**
Cooking oil	**3 tbsp.**	**45 mL**
Finely chopped onion	**3 tbsp.**	**45 mL**
Lemon juice	**2 tbsp.**	**30 mL**
Lime juice	**2 tbsp.**	**30 mL**
Orange juice	**2 tbsp.**	**30 mL**
Finely chopped jalapeño pepper (see sidebar, page 150)	**1 tbsp.**	**15 mL**
Chili powder	**1/2 tsp.**	**2 mL**
Salt	**1/2 tsp.**	**2 mL**
Pepper	**1/4 tsp.**	**1 mL**
Diced avocado	**3/4 cup**	**175 mL**
Diced fresh tomato	**3/4 cup**	**175 mL**
Chopped fresh cilantro	**1/4 cup**	**60 mL**

Pour water into a large saucepan. Bring to a boil. Add shrimp. Cook, uncovered, for about 1 minute until starting to turn pink. Drain. Plunge into ice water in a large bowl. Let stand until cool. Drain and coarsely chop shrimp.

Combine next 11 ingredients in a medium bowl. Add shrimp and toss gently. Chill, covered, for 1 hour to blend flavours.

Add remaining 3 ingredients. Toss gently. Makes about 4 3/4 cups (1.2 L).

Potluck suggestion: Can serve up to 10.

Summer Spinach Salad

Nothing says "summer" like fresh greens and fruit! The pumpkin and flax seeds are optional but give an appealing crunch.

Olive (or cooking) oil	**1/4 cup**	**60 mL**
Apple cider vinegar	**3 tbsp.**	**45 mL**
Liquid honey	**1 tbsp.**	**15 mL**
Chopped fresh mint leaves (or 3/4 tsp., 4 mL, dried)	**1 tbsp.**	**15 mL**
Salt, to taste		
Pepper, to taste		
Torn fresh spinach, lightly packed	**6 cups**	**1.5 L**
Paper-thin sliced red onion	**3/4 cup**	**175 mL**
Sliced fresh strawberries	**1 cup**	**250 mL**
Shelled pumpkin seeds (optional)	**3 tbsp.**	**45 mL**
Flax seeds (optional)	**2 tsp.**	**10 mL**

Combine first 6 ingredients in a small bowl or jar with a tight-fitting lid. Cover or seal. Stir or shake vigorously. Let stand for 30 minutes to blend flavors.

Combine remaining 5 ingredients in a large bowl. Shake vinaigrette. Drizzle over salad and toss lightly. Serve immediately. Makes 4 servings.

Having trouble with an errant tablecloth flapping around in the wind and knocking over the food on your picnic table? If it is a disposable tablecloth, tape it to the underside of the table with some sturdy duct tape. For a fancier tablecloth, try clipping the ends around the table legs with clothespins.

Chicken Taco Layers

This easy layered salad will be a sure hit. It features everyone's favourite Mexican flavours, all dressed in a delicious lime and sour cream blend.

Shredded iceberg lettuce, lightly packed	**4 cups**	**1 L**
Chopped cooked chicken	**2 cups**	**500 mL**
Medium salsa	**1/2 cup**	**125 mL**
Chopped avocado	**2 cups**	**500 mL**
Chopped tomato	**2 cups**	**500 mL**
Chopped green onion	**3/4 cup**	**175 mL**
Grated Mexican cheese blend	**1 cup**	**250 mL**
Sour cream	**1/2 cup**	**125 mL**
Chopped fresh jalapeño peppers (see sidebar, page 150)	**2 tbsp.**	**30 mL**
Lime juice	**2 tbsp.**	**30 mL**
Chopped fresh cilantro (or parsley)	**1 tbsp.**	**15 mL**
Olive (or cooking) oil	**1 tbsp.**	**15 mL**
Salt	**1/2 tsp.**	**2 mL**
Crushed tortilla chips	**1 cup**	**250 mL**

Arrange lettuce in an extra-large glass bowl.

Combine chicken and salsa in medium bowl. Spoon over lettuce.

Layer next 4 ingredients, in order given, over chicken mixture.

Process next 6 ingredients in a blender until smooth. Drizzle over cheese.

Scatter tortilla chips over top. Makes about 13 cups (3.25 L).

Potluck suggestion: Can serve up to 15.

Don't have any leftover chicken? Start with two boneless, skinless chicken breast halves (4 to 6 oz., 113 to 117 g, each). Place in a large frying pan with 1 cup (250 mL) water or chicken broth. Simmer, covered, for 12 to 14 minutes until no longer pink inside. Drain. Chop. Makes about 2 cups (500 mL) of cooked chicken.

Baked Brie

Rich and decadent, yet simple to prepare, this baked brie is served whole, warm from the oven with crackers. Your guests will never guess how little effort you put in for such irresistible results. The combination of light, flaky pastry and warm melted cheese is unbeatable.

Package of puff pastry (14 oz., 397 g), thawed according to package directions	**1/2**	**1/2**
Brie cheese round (1 lb., 454 g)	**1**	**1**
Dried blueberries	**1/4 cup**	**60 mL**
Dried cranberries	**1/4 cup**	**60 mL**
Egg yolk (large)	**1**	**1**
Water	**1 tsp.**	**5 mL**

Roll out puff pastry on a lightly floured surface to 12 x 12 inch (30 x 30 cm) square. Trim corners at an angle. Cut decorative shapes from trimmings.

Cut cheese round in half horizontally. Place 1 half, cut side up, in centre of pastry. Scatter blueberries and cranberries over cheese. Cover with remaining half, cut side down. Fold edges of pastry together over cheese to enclose. Press edges to seal. Place, seam side down, on a greased baking sheet with sides.

Combine egg yolk and water in a small bowl. Brush over pastry. Arrange decorative shapes over top. Brush with remaining egg yolk mixture. Cut 5 small vents in top to allow steam to escape. Bake on centre rack in 450°F (230°C) oven for about 15 minutes until pastry is golden brown. Let stand on baking sheet for 10 minutes. Makes 8 servings.

Potluck suggestion: Can serve up to 12.

Pumpkin and Herb Biscuits

These flakey, savoury biscuits are delicious on their own, spread with a little butter, or as an accompaniment to hearty autumn soups, stews or chilis—perfect for a Thanksgiving potluck! They are also a sophisticated option for the Thanksgiving table, nestled right alongside the traditional dinner buns.

All-purpose flour	**1 1/2 cups**	**375 mL**
Whole wheat flour	**1/2 cup**	**125 mL**
Baking powder	**1 tbsp.**	**15 mL**
Chopped fresh chives (or 2 1/4 tsp., 11 mL, dried)	**3 tbsp.**	**45 mL**
Chopped fresh thyme (or 3/4 tsp., 4 mL, dried)	**1 tbsp.**	**15 mL**
Ground nutmeg	**1/2 tsp.**	**2 mL**
Salt	**1/2 tsp.**	**2 mL**
Pepper	**1/2 tsp.**	**2 mL**
Large egg	**1**	**1**
Buttermilk	**1/2 cup**	**125 mL**
Canned pure pumpkin (no spices)	**1/2 cup**	**125 mL**
Cooking oil	**3 tbsp.**	**45 mL**
Large egg, fork-beaten	**1**	**1**

Combine first 8 ingredients in a large bowl. Make a well in centre.

Beat first egg with a fork in a medium bowl. Stir in next 3 ingredients. Add to well. Mix until soft dough forms. Do not overmix. Turn dough out onto lightly floured surface. Press out to 1 inch (2.5 cm) thickness. Cut with 2 inch (5 cm) round biscuit cutter. Arrange, almost touching, in greased 9 x 9 inch (23 x 23 cm) pan.

Brush tops with second egg. Bake in 475°F (240°C) oven for 12 to 15 minutes until golden. Makes about 12 biscuits.

Be careful to purchase the right type of canned pumpkin that your recipe calls for. Pure pumpkin is just that—pumpkin with nothing added. Pumpkin pie filling, on the other hand, is pumpkin that has been blended with sugar and spices.

Sweet Potato Casserole

The sweetness in this brown sugar-accented casserole is the perfect contrast for all those savoury Thanksgiving supper staples.

Large eggs, fork-beaten	**2**	**2**
Mashed sweet potatoes	**3 cups**	**750 mL**
Butter (or hard margarine), softened	**1/4 cup**	**60 mL**
Granulated sugar	**1/4 cup**	**60 mL**
Vanilla extract	**1 tsp.**	**5 mL**
Salt	**1/4 tsp.**	**1 mL**
Butter (or hard margarine)	**1/4 cup**	**60 mL**
Brown sugar, packed	**1/2 cup**	**125 mL**
Chopped pecans	**1/2 cup**	**125 mL**
All-purpose flour	**1/4 cup**	**60 mL**

Combine first 6 ingredients in a medium bowl. Transfer to a greased 2 quart (2 L) shallow baking dish.

Melt second amount of butter in a small saucepan on medium. Remove from heat. Add remaining 3 ingredients. Stir well. Sprinkle over sweet potato mixture. Bake, uncovered, in 350°F (175°C) oven for about 30 minutes until golden. Makes 8 servings.

If you have to transport your casserole to your Thanksgiving get-together, wrap a thick rubber band around each casserole handle and criss-cross them around the lid handle to keep it in place. If your casserole doesn't have handles, cover it with foil to secure the lid.

Sweet Saffron Pilaf

Saffron can be a little expensive, but the aromatic flavour and intense colour it adds are worth every penny and add a dramatic flair to your Thanksgiving table. Nuts and fruit add flavour to this convenient rice dish that bakes in the oven to a golden finish. You can assemble the pilaf in the baking dish up to 8 hours ahead of time, then cover and chill until you are ready to bake it. Increase the baking time by 10 minutes.

Warm water	**1 tbsp.**	**15 mL**
Saffron threads	**1/4 tsp.**	**1 mL**
Water	**8 cups**	**2 L**
Salt	**2 tsp.**	**10 mL**
White basmati (or long-grain) rice	**1 1/2 cups**	**375 mL**
Butter (or hard margarine)	**2 tbsp.**	**30 mL**
Finely chopped onion	**1/2 cup**	**125 mL**
Chopped pistachios	**1/2 cup**	**125 mL**
Chopped dried apricot	**1/4 cup**	**60 mL**
Dried cranberries	**1/4 cup**	**60 mL**
Liquid honey	**1/4 cup**	**60 mL**
Grated orange zest	**1 tbsp.**	**15 mL**

Combine warm water and saffron in a small bowl. Set aside.

Combine second amount of water and salt in a Dutch oven or large pot. Bring to a boil. Stir in rice. Reduce heat to medium. Cook, uncovered, for about 15 minutes, stirring occasionally, until rice is tender. Drain. Rinse with cold water. Drain well. Set aside.

Melt butter in a large frying pan on medium. Add onion and cook for about 5 minutes, stirring often, until softened.

Add remaining 5 ingredients and saffron mixture. Heat, stirring, for 1 minute. Remove from heat. Stir in rice. Spread rice mixture evenly in a greased 2 quart (2 L) shallow baking dish. Bake, uncovered, in 375°F (190°C) oven for about 25 minutes until rice is heated through and edges are golden. Makes about 6 cups (1.5 L).

Greasing the baking dish with butter will result in a delicious, crusty browned rice edge.

Fruity Coleslaw

Another fan favourite, this recipe first appeared in Potluck Dishes. *Crispy, crunchy and sweet, it is a pleasant change from traditional coleslaw. Apples are at their best in autumn and really add a bright, fresh flavour to this salad.*

Shredded green cabbage, lightly packed	**5 cups**	**1.25 L**
Shredded red cabbage, lightly packed	**3 cups**	**750 mL**
Can of mandarin orange segments (10 oz., 284 mL), drained	**1**	**1**
Medium cooking apple (such as McIntosh), with peel, core removed, diced (about 1 cup, 250 mL)	**1**	**1**
Sour cream	**1 cup**	**250 mL**
Orange juice	**1/4 cup**	**60 mL**
Liquid honey	**2 tbsp.**	**30 mL**
Grated orange zest	**1/2 tsp.**	**2 mL**
Celery seed	**1/2 tsp.**	**2 mL**
Salt	**1/2 tsp.**	**2 mL**
Pepper	**1/4 tsp.**	**1 mL**

Put first 4 ingredients into an extra-large bowl. Toss lightly.

Combine remaining 7 ingredients in a small bowl. Drizzle over salad and toss well. Chill, covered, for at least 2 hours until cold. Remove salad with slotted spoon to a large serving bowl. Discard any excess liquid. Makes 12 servings.

To reduce congestion at the buffet table, consider preparing little cutlery bundles that your guests can quickly and easily pick up as they enter or exit the area. Wrap the cutlery in a napkin and secure it with a rubber band or, for a more attractive presentation, some colourful string or ribbon tied with a decorative bow.

Happy Thanksgiving

Pancetta and Pine Nut Brussels Sprouts

Because they have such a bad rap, Brussels sprouts might seem like a risky choice for a party or potluck, but once they taste this dish, your guests will gain a new appreciation for this much-maligned veggie. Paired with crispy pancetta and baked to perfection, these sprouts are outstanding.

Brussels sprouts	**2 lbs.**	**900 g**
Olive oil	**1 tsp.**	**5 mL**
Pancetta, diced	**5 oz.**	**140 g**
Salt, to taste		
Pepper, to taste		
Pine nuts, toasted (see sidebar, page 70)	**1/2 cup**	**125 mL**

Preheat oven to 400°F (200°C). Slice the Brussels sprouts in half lengthwise, removing any loose, outer leaves and trimming the bottom stems. Toss in olive oil and add pancetta, salt and pepper. Spread in a single layer on a baking sheet and bake for 20 to 30 minutes until pancetta is crispy. Stir occasionally, so the Brussels sprouts cook evenly.

Toss with the pine nuts. Makes 6 servings.

Potluck suggestion: Can serve up to 10.

Orange Balsamic Beets

Roasting whole beets takes time, but the sweet natural flavour, complemented by a tangy-sweet sauce is well worth it. Place them in the oven alongside the turkey.

Fresh medium beets, scrubbed clean and trimmed	**2 lbs.**	**900 g**
Medium onion (with skin)	**1**	**1**
Orange juice	**1/2 cup**	**125 mL**
Balsamic vinegar	**1/3 cup**	**75 mL**
Brown sugar, packed	**1 tbsp.**	**15 mL**
Star anise	**1**	**1**
Salt	**1/8 tsp.**	**0.5 mL**
Pepper	**1/8 tsp.**	**0.5 mL**

Place each beet on a small sheet of greased heavy-duty (or a double layer of regular) foil. Fold edges over beet to enclose. Place onion on a small sheet of greased heavy-duty (or a double layer of regular) foil. Fold edges of foil together over onion to enclose. Place on centre rack in 400°F (200°C) oven. Cook beets for about 1 hour and 20 minutes and onion for about 1 hour until tender. Transfer to a cutting board. Carefully remove foil. Let stand until cool enough to handle. Peel beets and cut each into 8 wedges. Peel onion. Cut in half and then into thin slices.

Combine remaining 6 ingredients in a medium saucepan. Bring to a boil. Reduce heat to medium. Cook, uncovered, for about 10 minutes, stirring occasionally, until reduced by half. Remove and discard star anise. Add beet and onion. Stir until heated through. Makes about 5 1/2 cups (1.4 L).

Gingersnap Pumpkin Cheesecake

Give the traditional pumpkin pie a rest this Thanksgiving and serve up this scrumptious cheesecake instead. Garnish with pipes of whipped cream for an even lovelier presentation. This cheesecake must be chilled for at least 6 hours, so plan accordingly.

Butter (or hard margarine)	**1/4 cup**	**60 mL**
Finely crushed gingersnap cookies	**1 1/4 cups**	**300 mL**
Blocks of cream cheese (8 oz., 250 g, each), softened	**2**	**2**
Granulated sugar	**2/3 cup**	**150 mL**
Large eggs	**2**	**2**
Can of pure pumpkin (no spices), 14 oz., 398 mL (see sidebar, page 108)	**1**	**1**
Ground cinnamon	**1/2 tsp.**	**2 mL**
Ground ginger	**1/2 tsp.**	**2 mL**
Ground nutmeg	**1/2 tsp.**	**2 mL**
Salt	**1/2 tsp.**	**2 mL**

Melt butter in a medium saucepan. Remove from heat. Stir in cookie crumbs. Press firmly in an ungreased 9 inch (23 cm) springform pan. Bake in 350°F (175°C) oven for 10 minutes. Let stand until cool.

For the filling, beat cream cheese and sugar in a large bowl until smooth. Add eggs, 1 at a time, beating after each addition until just combined.

Add remaining 5 ingredients. Beat well. Spread evenly over crust. Bake for 50 to 60 minutes until centre is almost set. Run knife around inside edge of pan to allow cheesecake to settle evenly. Let stand in pan on a wire rack until cooled completely. Chill for at least 6 hours or overnight. Cuts into 12 wedges.

Potluck suggestion: Can serve up to 18.

Pear Cranberry Crumble

Fresh fruit always tastes best in season, and pears are at their best in autumn. Juicy and sweet, they pair perfectly with tart cranberries in this delicious crumble. This warm, comforting dessert merits a place on the Thanksgiving dinner table, right next to the pumpkin pie.

Peeled pears, cores removed and sliced	**3**	**3**
Bag of fresh (or frozen, thawed) cranberries (12 oz., 340 g)	**1**	**1**
Brown sugar, packed	**1/2 cup**	**125 mL**
Minute tapioca	**3 tbsp.**	**45 mL**
Lemon juice	**2 tsp.**	**10 mL**
All-bran cereal	**2/3 cup**	**150 mL**
Quick-cooking rolled oats	**2/3 cup**	**150 mL**
Brown sugar, packed	**1/3 cup**	**75 mL**
Ground ginger	**1/2 tsp.**	**2 mL**
Ground cinnamon	**1/4 tsp.**	**1 mL**
Butter (or hard margarine), cut up	**1/2 cup**	**125 mL**
Vanilla ice cream (optional)		

Combine first 5 ingredients in a medium bowl. Spread evenly in a greased shallow 2 quart (2 L) baking dish.

Combine next 5 ingredients in a large bowl. Cut in butter until mixture resembles coarse crumbs. Sprinkle evenly over pear mixture. Bake in 375°F (190°C) oven for 40 to 45 minutes until pear is tender and topping is browned. Let stand for 15 minutes.

Serve warm with ice cream. Makes 6 servings.

Bat Wings

Okay so they are actually chicken wings, not bat wings, but they are so cheesy and delicious that they are sure to fly off the plate at your next Halloween get-together.

Plain yogurt	**1/2 cup**	**125 mL**
Lemon juice	**3 tbsp.**	**45 mL**
Prepared mustard	**2 tsp.**	**10 mL**
Prepared horseradish	**1/4 tsp.**	**1 mL**
Garlic powder	**1/4 tsp.**	**1 mL**
Ground thyme	**1/4 tsp.**	**1 mL**
Turmeric	**1/4 tsp.**	**1 mL**
Dry fine bread crumbs	**1/3 cup**	**75 mL**
Grated Parmesan cheese	**2/3 cup**	**150 mL**
Salt	**1 tsp.**	**5 mL**
Chicken drumettes (or whole wings)	**2 lbs.**	**900 g**

Mix first 7 ingredients in a bowl.

Mix bread crumbs, cheese and salt in a second bowl.

Add drumettes to yogurt mixture (if using whole wings, first discard tips and cut wings apart at joint). Stir to coat. Marinate in refrigerator for 2 to 3 hours or longer. Remove from marinade and drain. Roll in cheese mixture and place on a greased tray lined with foil. Bake in 350°F (175°C) oven for about 45 minutes until tender. Serve hot. Makes about 16 drumettes or 24 pieces of whole wings.

Devil's Dip

Serve this special dip hot from the oven and watch it disappear. Devilishly delicious, it pairs well with whole-grain crackers, tortilla chips, pita bread or slices of fresh baguette.

Cream cheese, softened	**8 oz.**	**250 g**
Sour cream	**1 cup**	**250 mL**
Container of jalepeño bean dip (10.5 oz., 298 g)	**1**	**1**
Drops of tabasco	**10**	**10**
Dried chives	**3 tbsp.**	**45 mL**
Parsley flakes	**2 tsp.**	**10 mL**
Chili powder	**1 tsp.**	**5 mL**
Grated Monterey Jack cheese	**1 1/2 cups**	**375 mL**
Grated medium Cheddar cheese	**1 1/2 cups**	**375 mL**
Chili powder, sprinkle		

Mix first 6 ingredients together. Spread in 9 x 13 inch (23 x 33 cm) pan.

Sprinkle first amount of chili powder over top, adding more if necessary to cover. Add a layer of Monterey Jack cheese, then a layer of Cheddar cheese. Sprinkle with second amount of chili powder. Bake in 350°F (175°C) oven for about 20 minutes or up to 40 minutes for a crispy effect. Makes 4 cups (500 mL).

Witches' Fingers

There's something deliciously depraved about munching on these sweet, crunchy fingers. A perfect offering for your next Halloween bash—for kids or adults. Make the cookies narrower than you think they should be, as they will spread during baking.

All-purpose flour	**2 1/2 cups**	**625 mL**
Baking powder	**1 tsp.**	**5 mL**
Salt	**1 tsp.**	**5 mL**
Butter, softened	**1 cup**	**250 mL**
Granulated sugar	**1 cup**	**250 mL**
Large egg	**1**	**1**
Almond extract	**1 tsp.**	**5 mL**
Vanilla extract	**1 tsp.**	**5 mL**
Whole blanched almonds	**1/2 cup**	**125 mL**
Red or green food coloring (optional)		

Combine flour, baking powder and salt in a mixing bowl.

In another large bowl, beat together butter, sugar, egg, and almond and vanilla extracts. Beat in dry ingredients until dough is well mixed. Cover and refrigerate dough for 30 minutes. Divide dough into 4 sections. Keep remaining dough refrigerated as you work on first section. Roll small balls of dough (about 2 tbsp., 30 mL) into finger shapes. Squeeze dough in a couple of spots to form appearance of knuckles.

Press an almond firmly onto one end of each finger to form fingernails. Paint each almond with red or green food coloring, if desired. Place cookies on a lightly greased cookie sheet and bake in 325°F (160°C) oven for 20 to 25 minutes or until golden. Let cool for 2 to 3 minutes before removing to a wire rack to cool. Makes about 36 cookies.

You can lift up the almonds on the baked cookies and squeeze some red decorating gel under each nail. Press the almond back in place so that the gel oozes out. You can also add green food coloring to the dough to make green witches' fingers.

Crispy Jerk Chicken Rolls

Next time you get together with the gang to cheer on your favourite team, offer up a plate of these chicken rolls. Crispy with a nice amount of spice, they make a nice change from the traditional fare served at Grey Cup parties.

Cooking oil	**2 tsp.**	**10 mL**
Chopped onion	**2 cups**	**500 mL**
Grated carrot	**2 cups**	**500 mL**
Chopped pickled jalapeño pepper (see sidebar, page 150)	**2 tbsp.**	**30 mL**
Jerk paste	**2 1/2 tsp.**	**12 mL**
Garlic cloves, minced	**2**	**2**
Ground allspice	**1/4 tsp.**	**1 mL**
Chopped cooked chicken	**2 cups**	**500 mL**
Plain yogurt	**1/4 cup**	**60 mL**
Spring roll wrappers (6 inch, 15 cm, square)	**16**	**16**
Egg whites (large)	**1**	**1**
Water	**1 tbsp.**	**15 mL**
Cooking oil	**3 cups**	**750 mL**

Heat first amount of cooking oil in a large frying pan on medium. Add next 6 ingredients. Cook, stirring often, for about 10 minutes until onion is softened.

Stir in chicken and yogurt.

Arrange wrappers on a work surface. Combine egg whites and water in a small cup. Place about 1/4 cup (60 mL) chicken mixture near bottom right corner of each wrapper. Fold corner up and over filling. Fold in sides. Dampen edges with egg white mixture. Roll up to opposite corner. Press to seal.

Heat second amount of cooking oil in a large frying pan on medium-high. Shallow-fry 2 or 3 rolls at a time, turning often, until golden. Transfer to paper towels to drain. Makes 16 rolls.

Avocado Bacon Triangles

These delicious triangles with bacon, tomato and a lemony avocado spread have intense flavour that is reminiscent of a BLT. A single batch may not be enough.

Whole wheat (or white) bread slices, crusts removed	**6**	**6**
Cooking oil	**2 tbsp.**	**30 mL**
Mashed avocado	**3/4 cup**	**175 mL**
Block cream cheese, softened	**1/3 cup**	**75 mL**
Sun-dried tomatoes in oil, blotted dry, finely chopped	**1/4 cup**	**60 mL**
Dijon mustard	**1 tbsp.**	**15 mL**
Lemon juice	**1 tbsp.**	**15 mL**
Pepper	**1/4 tsp.**	**1 mL**
Finely diced seeded tomato	**1/2 cup**	**125 mL**
Bacon slices, cooked crisp and crumbled	**6**	**6**
Finely chopped chives	**1 tbsp.**	**15 mL**

Brush bread slices with cooking oil. Cut each slice diagonally into 4 triangles. Arrange on a greased baking sheet with sides. Broil on top rack in oven for 1 to 2 minutes per side until golden.

Combine next 6 ingredients in a small bowl. Spread over triangles.

Sprinkle with remaining 3 ingredients. Makes 24 triangles.

Chorizo Chili

Nothing hits the spot on Grey Cup day like a bowl of piping hot chili. Garnish individual servings with a dollop of sour cream and finely diced red onion. The spicy flavors are perfect with an ice-cold beer.

Ingredient	Imperial	Metric
Cooking oil	**2 tsp.**	**10 mL**
Chopped onion	**1 cup**	**250 mL**
Medium red pepper, diced	**1**	**1**
Garlic clove, minced (or 1/4 tsp., 1 mL, powder)	**1**	**1**
Lean ground beef	**1 lb.**	**454 g**
Chili sauce	**3/4 cup**	**175 mL**
Chili powder	**1 tbsp.**	**15 mL**
Beef bouillon powder	**1 tbsp.**	**15 mL**
Paprika	**1 tbsp.**	**15 mL**
Dried whole oregano	**1 tbsp.**	**15 mL**
Ground cumin	**1 tsp.**	**5 mL**
Cayenne pepper	**1/4 tsp.**	**1 mL**
Pepper	**1 tsp.**	**5 mL**
Cans of diced tomatoes, with juice (14 oz., 398 mL, each)	**2**	**2**
Beer	**1 cup**	**250 mL**
Can of tomato paste (5 1/2 oz., 156 mL)	**1**	**1**
Bay leaf	**1**	**1**
Cooked chorizo sausage, cut into 1/4 inch (6 mm) slices (about 3 cups, 750 mL)	**1 lb.**	**454 g**
Can of black beans (19 oz., 540 mL), drained and rinsed	**1**	**1**

Heat oil in a large pot or Dutch oven on medium. Add onion, red pepper and garlic and cook until onion is soft.

Add ground beef. Scramble-fry for about 5 minutes until beef is no longer pink. Drain.

Stir in next 8 ingredients. Cook for 3 minutes to blend flavors.

Stir in tomatoes, beer, tomato paste and bay leaf. Bring to a boil. Reduce heat and simmer, covered, for 1 1/2 hours, stirring occasionally. Remove and discard bay leaf.

Stir in sausage and beans. Simmer, uncovered, for about 30 minutes until thickened. Makes 8 cups (2 L).

Toffee Bar Cookies

Satisfy everyone's sweet tooth with these chocolate and toffee cookies. Good thing this recipe makes a lot of cookies—you'll need them! Or make giant cookies by rolling the dough into 2 inch (5 cm) balls and arranging them 4 inches (10 cm) apart on the cookie sheet.

Ingredient	Imperial	Metric
Butter (or hard margarine), softened	**1 cup**	**250 mL**
Brown sugar, packed	**1 cup**	**250 mL**
Granulated sugar	**1 cup**	**250 mL**
Large eggs	**2**	**2**
Vanilla extract	**2 tsp.**	**10 mL**
All-purpose flour	**2 cups**	**500 mL**
Baking powder	**1 tsp.**	**5 mL**
Baking soda	**1 tsp.**	**5 mL**
Salt	**1/2 tsp.**	**2 mL**
Quick-cooking rolled oats	**2 1/3 cups**	**575 mL**
Chocolate-covered buttery toffee bars (1 1/2 oz., 39 g, each), coarsely chopped	**8**	**8**

Cream first 3 ingredients in a large bowl. Add eggs 1 at a time, beating well after each addition. Add vanilla. Beat until smooth.

Combine next 4 ingredients in a small bowl. Add to butter mixture in 2 additions, mixing well after each addition until no dry flour remains.

Add rolled oats and chocolate bar pieces. Mix well. Roll into 1 inch (2.5 cm) balls. Arrange about 2 inches (5 cm) apart on greased cookie sheets.

Flatten balls to 1/2 inch (12 mm) thickness. Bake in 375°F (190°C) oven for 10 to 12 minutes until golden. Let stand on cookie sheets for 5 minutes before removing to wire racks to cool. Makes about 72 cookies.

Sesame Shrimp Sushi Rolls

These delicately flavoured rolls are the perfect appetizer for a Christmas get-together, offering a lighter, healthier choice at a time when heavy, calorie-laden foods predominate.

Water	**2 1/4 cups**	**550 mL**
Short-grain white rice, rinsed and drained	**1 1/2 cups**	**375 mL**
Rice vinegar	**2 tbsp.**	**30 mL**
Granulated sugar	**1 tbsp.**	**15 mL**
Salt	**1/4 tsp.**	**1 mL**
Peeled orange-fleshed sweet potato sticks (1/2 x 4 inch, 12 mm x 10 cm, pieces)	**8**	**8**
Sesame (or cooking) oil	**2 tsp.**	**10 mL**
Nori (roasted seaweed) sheets	**4**	**4**
Cooked medium shrimp (peeled and deveined), halved lengthwise	**20**	**20**
Sesame and ginger salad dressing	**2 tbsp.**	**30 mL**
Julienned English cucumber (with peel)	**1/2 cup**	**125 mL**
Roasted sesame seeds	**1/4 cup**	**60 mL**

Pour water into a small saucepan and bring to a boil. Stir in rice. Reduce heat to medium-low and simmer, covered, for 20 minutes, without stirring. Remove from heat. Let stand, covered, for about 10 minutes until rice is tender and liquid is absorbed. Transfer to a large bowl.

Stir next 3 ingredients in a small bowl until sugar is dissolved. Stir into rice. Set aside to cool.

Brush both sides of sweet potato with sesame oil. Arrange in a greased pie plate. Cook in 425°F (220°C) oven for 10 to 12 minutes until tender-crisp. Set aside to cool.

Place 1 nori sheet, shiny side down, on a work surface. Spread about 1 cup (250 mL) rice mixture over nori, leaving a 2 inch (5 cm) border on top edge. Place 2 sweet potato sticks across rice mixture, about 2 inches (5 cm) from bottom edge.

Toss shrimp and salad dressing in a medium bowl. Arrange 1/4 of shrimp mixture and 1/4 of cucumber beside sweet potato. Sprinkle with 1 tbsp. (15 mL) sesame seeds. Dampen top edge of nori with water. Roll up tightly from bottom to enclose filling. Wrap in plastic wrap. Repeat with remaining ingredients. Chill for about 1 hour until firm. Discard plastic wrap. Trim ends. Cut each roll into 8 slices. Makes 32 rolls.

To julienne, cut into very thin strips that resemble matchsticks.

Onion Pepper Phyllo Squares

These elegant squares are sophisticated enough to warrant a place of honour on the Christmas buffet table. Sweet onion, peppers and cheese top a crisp, flaky crust for an appetizer that is as pleasing to the eye as it is to the taste buds.

Cooking oil	**1 tbsp.**	**15 mL**
Thinly sliced onion	**2 cups**	**500 mL**
Garlic cloves, minced (or 1/2 tsp., 2 mL, powder)	**2**	**2**
Liquid honey	**1 1/2 tsp.**	**7 mL**
Dried crushed chilies	**1 tsp.**	**5 mL**
Frozen phyllo pastry sheets, thawed according to package directions	**12**	**12**
Butter (or hard margarine), melted	**1/2 cup**	**125 mL**
Thinly sliced roasted red peppers (or 1/2 of 13 oz., 370 mL, jar, drained and thinly sliced)	**1/2 cup**	**125 mL**
Part-skim mozzarella cheese, thinly sliced	**8 oz.**	**225 g**
Torn fresh basil	**2 tbsp.**	**30 mL**
Finely grated fresh Parmesan cheese	**1/2 cup**	**125 mL**

Heat cooking oil in a large frying pan on medium. Add onion and cook for 12 to 15 minutes, stirring often, until soft and golden.

Add garlic, honey and chilies. Cook, stirring constantly, for about 2 minutes until fragrant. Let stand until slightly cooled.

Work with phyllo sheets 1 at a time. Keep remaining sheets covered with a damp tea towel to prevent drying. Lay 1 pastry sheet on a work surface and brush with melted butter. Lay second pastry sheet on top. Brush with melted butter. Repeat with remaining pastry sheets and melted butter. Carefully lift pastry layers into a greased 10 x 15 inch (25 x 38 cm) jelly roll pan. Press into corners and up sides of pan.

Scatter onion mixture, red peppers and mozzarella cheese slices over pastry. Sprinkle with basil and Parmesan cheese. Bake in 375°F (190°C) oven for 15 to 20 minutes until pastry is golden and crisp. Pastry may puff during baking but will deflate once removed from oven. Cuts into 8 squares.

Potluck suggestion: Can cut into up to 12 squares.

Spinach Chicken Lasagna

With plenty of sauce, rich flavours and a tempting appearance, this dish is sure to be a hit at your next Christmas potluck. In keeping with the season, you could substitute turkey breast for the chicken, if you prefer.

Spinach lasagna noodles	**12**	**12**
Cooking oil	**1 1/2 tbsp.**	**22 mL**
Boneless, skinless chicken breast halves, chopped	**1 3/4 lbs.**	**790 g**
Sliced fresh white mushrooms	**2 cups**	**500 mL**
Chopped onion	**1 1/2 cups**	**375 mL**
Chopped red pepper	**1 1/2 cups**	**375 mL**
Garlic cloves, minced (or 1/2 tsp., 2 mL, powder)	**2**	**2**
Tomato pasta sauce	**4 cups**	**1 L**
Chopped fresh spinach leaves, lightly packed	**2 cups**	**500 mL**
Can of diced tomatoes (14 oz., 398 mL), with juice	**1**	**1**
Dried oregano	**2 tsp.**	**10 mL**
Dried basil	**1 tsp.**	**5 mL**
Salt	**1/4 tsp.**	**1 mL**
Pepper	**1/8 tsp.**	**0.5 mL**
Cayenne pepper (optional)	**1/4 tsp.**	**1 mL**
2% cottage cheese	**1 1/2 cups**	**375 mL**
Crumbled feta cheese	**1/2 cup**	**125 mL**
Grated Parmesan cheese	**1/3 cup**	**75 mL**
Dried thyme	**1/2 tsp.**	**2 mL**
Pepper	**1/2 tsp.**	**2 mL**
Dried rosemary, crushed	**1/4 tsp.**	**1 mL**
Grated mozzarella and Cheddar cheese blend	**2 cups**	**500 mL**
Parsley flakes	**2 tsp.**	**10 mL**

Cook lasagna noodles according to package directions. Drain well and set aside to cool.

Heat cooking oil in same pot on medium-high. Add chicken and cook for 8 to 10 minutes, stirring occasionally, until no longer pink. Remove to a plate. Reduce heat to medium.

Add next 4 ingredients to same pot. Cook for about 10 minutes, stirring often, until onion is softened.

Stir in next 8 ingredients and chicken. Simmer, covered, for 10 minutes, stirring occasionally, to blend flavours. Remove from heat. Set aside.

Combine next 6 ingredients in a medium bowl.

To assemble, layer ingredients in a greased 9 x 13 inch (23 x 33 cm) baking pan as follows: 1 cup (250 mL) chicken mixture, 3 lasagna noodles, 3 cups (750 mL) chicken mixture, 3 lasagna noodles, cottage cheese mixture, 3 lasagna noodles, 3 cups (750 mL) chicken mixture, 3 lasagna noodles and remaining chicken mixture

Combine cheese blend and parsley in a medium bowl. Sprinkle over top. Cover with greased foil and bake in 350°F (175°F) oven for 60 minutes. Remove foil and bake for another 30 minutes until cheese is bubbling and starting to turn golden. Let stand for 10 minutes before serving. Makes 8 servings.

Potluck suggestion: Can serve up to 12.

Lazy Perogy Casserole

Store-bought perogies cannot compare to homemade, but unless you have a room full of babcias to lend a hand, who has time around the holidays to spend on such an undertaking? Thankfully this simple casserole has all the same great flavour, without all the fuss! Serve with a dollop of sour cream.

Lasagna noodles	**15**	**15**
Large egg	**1**	**1**
2% cottage cheese	**2 cups**	**500 mL**
Onion salt	**1/4 tsp.**	**1 mL**
Mashed potatoes (about 1 lb., 454 g, uncooked)	**2 cups**	**500 mL**
Grated medium Cheddar cheese	**1 cup**	**250 mL**
Onion salt	**1/4 tsp.**	**1 mL**
Salt	**1/4 tsp.**	**1 mL**
Pepper	**1/8 tsp.**	**0.5 mL**
Butter (or hard margarine)	**1/2 cup**	**125 mL**
Chopped onion	**1 cup**	**250 mL**

Cook noodles in boiling salted water in uncovered Dutch oven for 12 to 14 minutes, stirring occasionally, until tender but firm. Drain and set aside.

Combine next 3 ingredients in a small bowl. Set aside.

Combine next 5 ingredients in a medium bowl. Set aside.

Melt butter in a medium frying pan. Add onion and cook on medium for about 10 minutes, stirring often, until very soft. Layer ingredients in a greased 9 x 13 inch (23 x 33 cm) pan as follows: 5 lasagna noodles, cottage cheese mixture, 5 lasagna noodles, potato mixture, 5 lasagna noodles, onion mixture. Cover with greased foil. Bake in 350°F (175°C) oven for 30 to 40 minutes until heated through. Let stand for 10 minutes before serving. Makes 8 servings.

Potluck suggestion: Can serve up to 12.

Walnut Cranberry Salad

This is a great salad for a potluck supper, especially as an accompaniment to lean cuts of meat such as chicken breasts or pork tenderloin. Baby spinach leaves are also good with this dressing, which is best made a little ahead of time so the flavours can develop.

Bags of baby greens (4 1/2 oz., 125 g, each), about 8 cups (2 L)	**2**	**2**
Walnuts, coarsely chopped	**1/2 cup**	**125 mL**
Dried cranberries	**1/2 cup**	**125 mL**
Goat cheese, crumbled (about 3/4 cup, 175 mL)	**4 1/2 oz.**	**125 g**
Bacon slices, cooked crisp and crumbled	**6**	**6**
Olive (or cooking) oil	**1/3 cup**	**75 mL**
White wine vinegar	**3 tbsp.**	**45 mL**
Brown sugar, packed	**1 tbsp.**	**15 mL**
Chopped fresh oregano leaves	**1 tbsp.**	**15 mL**
Prepared mustard	**2 tsp.**	**10 mL**
Garlic clove, crushed	**1**	**1**
Salt	**1/4 tsp.**	**1 mL**
Pepper	**1/4 tsp.**	**1 mL**

Combine first 3 ingredients in a large bowl. Sprinkle cheese and bacon over top.

For the dressing, combine remaining 8 ingredients in a small jar with a tight-fitting lid. Shake well to combine. Drizzle over salad and toss until evenly coated. Makes 10 cups (2.5 L).

Potluck suggestion: Can serve up to 10.

Cheesecake Brownie Bites

During the holidays when calorie-laden baked goods are at every turn, these cute bite-sized brownies are sure to be a hit. They are just enough of a good thing to satisfy without being overwhelming. For an extra festive touch, you could add some red or green food colouring to the icing.

All-purpose flour	**1/3 cup**	**75 mL**
Cocoa, sifted if lumpy	**1/3 cup**	**75 mL**
Salt	**1/8 tsp.**	**0.5 mL**
Large egg	**1**	**1**
Granulated sugar	**1/2 cup**	**125 mL**
Butter (or hard margarine), melted	**1/4 cup**	**60 mL**
Vanilla extract	**1/2 tsp.**	**2 mL**
Block cream cheese, cut up and softened	**4 oz.**	**125 g**
Icing (confectioner's) sugar	**1/4 cup**	**60 mL**
Grated orange zest	**1/2 tsp.**	**2 mL**

Combine first 3 ingredients in a small bowl.

Beat next 4 ingredients in a medium bowl. Add flour mixture and stir until just moistened. Fill 12 greased mini-muffin cups about 3/4 full. Bake in 350°F (175°C) oven for about 12 minutes until a wooden pick inserted in centre of brownie comes out moist but not wet with batter. Do not overbake. Let stand in pan for 5 minutes. Dent top of each brownie with your thumb. Transfer to a wire rack to cool.

Combine remaining 3 ingredients in a small bowl. Transfer to a piping bag or a small resealable freezer bag with a tiny piece snipped off 1 corner. Pipe into dents in brownies. Makes 12 brownies.

To make things easier for yourself on the day of your get-together, bake these brownies in advance and freeze them uniced. A few hours before you plan on serving them, take them out of the freezer and allow them to thaw, then add the icing.

Skinny Seven-layer Dip

Who doesn't love a good seven-layer dip? In this healthier take on the original, we've lowered the fat and sodium content, so you can get a head start on your New Year's resolution to eat a little healthier. Feel free to indulge without all the guilt. Scoop up the creamy goodness with baked tortilla chips.

Ingredient	Imperial	Metric
Can of romano beans, rinsed and drained (19 oz., 540 mL)	**1**	**1**
Canola oil	**1 tbsp.**	**15 mL**
Water	**1 tbsp.**	**15 mL**
Chili powder	**2 tsp.**	**10 mL**
Garlic clove, minced (or 1/4 tsp., 1 mL, powder)	**1**	**1**
Ground cumin	**1/4 tsp.**	**1 mL**
Chopped fresh spinach leaves, lightly packed	**1 cup**	**250 mL**
Non-fat plain yogurt	**1 cup**	**250 mL**
Hot salsa	**1/4 cup**	**60 mL**
Grated Mexican cheese blend	**2/3 cup**	**150 mL**
Diced avocado	**1 cup**	**250 mL**
Finely chopped pickled jalapeño peppers	**1 tbsp.**	**15 mL**
Lime juice	**1 tbsp.**	**15 mL**
Diced seeded Roma (plum) tomato	**1 cup**	**250 mL**
Thinly sliced green onion	**2 tbsp.**	**30 mL**
Chopped fresh cilantro (or parsley)	**1 tbsp.**	**15 mL**

Process first 6 ingredients in a blender or food processor until almost smooth. Spread evenly in an ungreased 9 inch (23 cm) pie plate.

Scatter spinach over bean mixture.

Stir yogurt and salsa in a small bowl. Spread over spinach. Sprinkle with cheese.

Toss next 3 ingredients in a small bowl. Scatter over cheese.

Layer remaining 3 ingredients, in order given, over avocado mixture. Makes 10 servings.

Wear gloves and don't touch your face when chopping hot peppers, as the oily compounds, called capsaicin (kap-SAY-ih-sihn), permeate the skin and can cause a burning sensation.

Party Meatballs

Serve these flavour-packed meatballs on toothpicks to make it easier for your guests to pick them up. Although they are delicious on their own, you could also offer a selection of sauces on the side for dipping.

Dry bread crumbs	**2/3 cup**	**150 mL**
Salt	**1 1/2 tsp.**	**7 mL**
Garlic powder	**1/2 tsp.**	**2 mL**
Onion powder	**1/2 tsp.**	**2 mL**
Ground nutmeg	**1/4 tsp.**	**1 mL**
Pepper	**1/4 tsp.**	**1 mL**
Large egg, fork-beaten	**1**	**1**
Water	**1/4 cup**	**60 mL**
Ground beef	**1 lb.**	**454 g**
Ground turkey	**1 lb.**	**454 g**

In a large bowl, combine first 6 ingredients. Stir in egg and water.

Crumble beef and turkey over mixture and mix well. Shape in to 1 inch (2.5 cm) balls and place in a greased 9 x 13 (23 x 33 cm) baking pan. Bake, uncovered, in 350°F (175°C) oven for 15 to 18 minutes until meat is no longer pink. Makes about 80 meatballs.

Want to throw a New Year's Party without breaking the bank? Make it a potluck! Ask your guests to bring along their favourite appetizer to share, and you'll have enough food to feed your crowd with much less effort and expense.

Spinach-stuffed Shells

These cheesy shells make an excellent vegetarian option for a New Year's Eve get-together, but if you have some dedicated carnivores in the crowd, feel free to add ground beef to the tomato sauce.

Can of tomato paste (5 1/2 oz., 156 mL)	**1**	**1**
Water	**1 1/4 cups**	**300 mL**
Salt	**1/2 tsp.**	**2 mL**
Parsley flakes	**1 tsp.**	**5 mL**
Ground oregano	**1/2 tsp.**	**2 mL**
Garlic powder	**1/2 tsp.**	**2 mL**
Ground sweet basil	**1/2 tsp.**	**2 mL**
Jumbo pasta shells	**20**	**20**
Package of frozen chopped spinach, thawed and squeezed dry (10 oz., 300 g)	**1**	**1**
Cottage cheese	**1 cup**	**250 mL**
Grated mozzarella cheese	**1 cup**	**250 mL**
Grated Parmesan cheese	**2 tbsp.**	**30 mL**
Grated mozzarella cheese	**1/2 cup**	**125 mL**

Combine first 7 ingredients in a large bowl. Set aside.

Cook shells according to package directions. Drain and set aside.

Combine next 4 ingredients in a medium bowl. Transfer to a resealable bag with 1 corner snipped off and pipe mixture into shells.

Pour half of tomato sauce into a 9 x 9 inch (23 x 23 cm) baking dish. Arrange shells over sauce and spoon remaining sauce over top. Cook, covered, in 350°F (175°C) oven for 30 to 40 minutes until bubbly hot. Sprinkle with second amount of mozzarella. Makes 20 stuffed shells.

Always cook your dish completely before taking it to the potluck. Never transport partially cooked food and finish cooking it at your destination.

Tiramisu

Rich, creamy and decadent. It's hard to find a better dessert than tiramisu. If you'd rather make this an alcohol-free dessert, increase the amount of coffee to replace the Marsala wine.

Whipping cream	**1 cup**	**250 mL**
Mascarpone cheese	**2 cups**	**500 mL**
Granulated sugar	**1/3 cup**	**75 mL**
Marsala wine	**1 tbsp.**	**15 mL**
Cold strong prepared coffee	**1/2 cup**	**125 mL**
Marsala wine	**3 tbsp.**	**45 mL**
Granulated sugar	**2 tbsp.**	**30 mL**
Ladyfingers, approximately	**24**	**24**
Cocoa	**1 tbsp.**	**15 mL**

Beat whipping cream in a small bowl until soft peaks form.

Using same beaters, beat next 3 ingredients in a medium bowl until smooth. Fold in whipped cream.

Stir next 3 ingredients in a small shallow bowl until sugar is dissolved. Quickly dip half of ladyfingers into coffee mixture, 1 at a time, until partially soaked through. Arrange in a single layer in ungreased 8 x 8 inch (20 x 20 cm) baking dish, trimming to fit if necessary. Spread half of cheese mixture evenly over ladyfingers. Repeat with remaining ladyfingers, coffee mixture and cheese mixture.

Sift cocoa through a fine sieve over top. Chill, covered, for at least 4 hours or overnight. Cuts into 9 pieces.

Potluck suggestion: Can cut into up to 12 pieces.

Index

R

S

T

V

W